BREW

BETTER COFFEE AT HOME

by Brian W. Jones

Photographs by Lizzie Munro

DOVETAIL

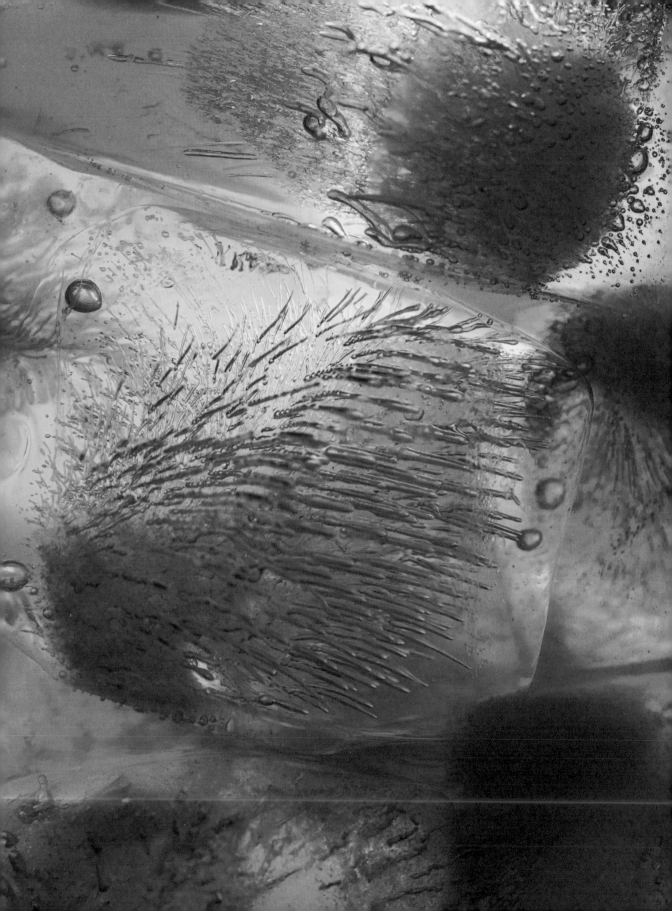

TABLE OF CONTENTS

INTRODUCTION

I love coffee. These days, I live coffee. I've worked as a barista and designed brands for renowned coffee companies. I now co-own a roasting company, and I travel the world writing about coffee culture. But, like many people, my relationship with the beverage has had its ups and downs. I remember tasting my parents' Maxwell House for the first time as a kid, then spending the next decade of my life thinking that coffee was the most vile beverage on Earth. No amount of sugar or milk made it remotely enjoyable.

By the time I reached high school I still wasn't drinking coffee, but I loved how it smelled as well as the social atmosphere a bustling coffee shop provided. This was during the peak of the *Friends* and *Seinfeld* era, when television's most influential characters spent most of their time in coffee shops. So I took my first barista job at a bookstore café in the hopes that I might learn to finally appreciate coffee. No such luck; even after learning how to brew a pot and pull a shot of espresso, I couldn't bring myself to drink coffee without adding a disproportionate amount of chocolate syrup and milk—you know, to help the medicine go down.

For years, a hit of caffeine was my sole reason for drinking coffee. After switching briefly to energy drinks in college, I returned to coffee once I entered the adult workforce, where the cultural prominence of the office coffee break prolonged my affair with a beverage that I still detested. It wasn't until a keen love interest of mine mentioned her attraction to guys who drank black coffee that I found the courage I needed to take my coffee unadulterated. At first it still tasted vile, and I despised every cup, but if it weren't for this masochistic habit inspired by my love for another person, I would have never fallen so hard for good coffee when I finally found it.

About a year into my torturous habit, I walked into a neighborhood café that served specialty coffee of the single-origin variety. I ordered my coffee black and stood by the window while it cooled. After I took my first sip, I waited for my face to twist from the bitterness, but it never happened. There was no burnt aroma, no ashy flavor, only a sweetness that reminded me of vanilla. I even asked the barista if I had been served the wrong drink, but I hadn't. I was truly enjoying my first cup of coffee, made with beans that came all the way from Ethiopia. I couldn't understand why this coffee tasted so incredibly different, and why, for the first time in my life, I actually enjoyed it sans milk. I was intent on learning more, and I have spent the last nine years doing just that. I hope that some of what I have learned will help you better understand and appreciate your own coffee and, most importantly, empower and excite you to brew better coffee at home.

Since the Boston Tea Party, the United States has been a country that favors coffee as its hot beverage of choice. But the beverage has come a long way from the pioneering days of gritty cowboy coffee and the freeze-dried instant coffee popularized by the soldiers returning from wars in the early twentieth century (what coffee people refer to as the "first wave"). When the 1970s arrived, the Mr. Coffee drip machine made its debut about the same time the first Starbucks opened in Seattle, marking the start of the "second wave." These new developments spurred not just the shift from instant coffee to home brewing, but the spread of Starbucks's version of the Italian-style café experience (and its espresso-based drinks) across America.

Now, a few decades later, good coffee has become increasingly accessible, and more specialty coffee shops are opening every week, all over the world (enter the "third wave"). More cities and towns have their own local roasters. More roasters are sourcing beans directly from farmers or through importers who offer more transparency about the whole process. Roasters are doing more to highlight the natural sweetness and nuanced flavors offered by different coffee beans. More experimentation and education has led to better brewing techniques that extract the best-tasting coffee. In short, there are more reasons than ever to fall in love with coffee, and this book will help you discover some of the many ways to make a delicious cup when you're away from your favorite barista or café.

Two diverging trends currently represent coffee brewing at home. You have the "slow coffee" movement, which includes a resurgence of manual coffee-brewing methods and equipment (pour over, French press, etc.) combined with fresh beans from small, quality-focused coffee-roasting companies. And then you have coffee pods and K-cups, which are essentially glorified means of making instant coffee. In this book, I focus on the slow coffee movement, in which quality trumps convenience.

Slow coffee isn't about the speed at which your coffee is brewed, but about the long journey that a quality coffee takes before arriving in your cup. There's a joy and satisfaction that comes with making a fresh cup of coffee at home that tastes just as good as one you can get in a great coffee shop. Unlike expensive espresso machines, the equipment you need for brewing slow coffee at home is rather affordable, and it takes only a few minutes to make great coffee. For me, waking up

and brewing my first cup of the day, or taking a coffee break from work in the afternoon, provides a calming routine that lets me take part in that long journey myself. When I'm brewing my own coffee, I know that I'm the last person in a long chain of people who have worked hard to make every drop as delicious as possible.

While many people have begun trying their hand at brewing beer, mixing cocktails, and cooking more ambitious recipes at home, there's also a growing number of folks who won't settle for subpar coffee, especially in their own domain. This book is for you. Likewise, many of us have purchased or been gifted various styles of brewing equipment—a French press, perhaps, or pour-over dripper, or even the mysterious AeroPress—but don't know how to get the best out of them. This book is for you as well.

While brewing coffee requires a bit of science, learning how to do it right doesn't require much scientific knowledge. But in order to make better coffee, it helps to understand where coffee beans come from, how they're processed and roasted, and, of course, the techniques required to brew a proper cup. In the following chapters, I'll cover all these topics, from bean to finished brew.

I begin with an overview of where coffee beans come from and how they find their way into your kitchen. In "The Bean," I will help you better understand the impact that a coffee's origin, processing, and roasting has on flavor. This information will help you decide what types of coffee beans you enjoy most and how to select them.

"The Brew" chapter covers what happens when you combine coffee beans with water. A bit of science and attention to technique will ensure that your coffee tastes great every time you brew it. I'll teach you some of the various slow coffee methods, both hot and cold, that you can use at home. "The Tools"

covers the equipment you need to execute them. Once you understand the basic brewing methods, you'll be able to decide which one is right for you, and which equipment to purchase and use.

After covering the essential brewing methods in detail, we'll end the journey with recipes to help you broaden your coffee-drinking horizons. I also include some ways to turn home-brewed coffee into a variety of coffee-based drinks, from cocktails to milkshakes. Experimentation and the joy of discovery are part of what makes doing things yourself so rewarding. So with the knowledge in this book and inspirational recipes as your guide, you'll be able to take your coffee consumption to new levels without having to leave your home.

This book is not intended to make you a professional coffee expert (though it might inspire you to take that path). Instead, it is a primer to provide you a better understanding of coffee: where it comes from, how to brew it better, and how to talk about it with more confidence. In the end, I want nothing more than for you to enjoy better coffee as soon and as often as possible.

AN INCREDIBLY BRIEF HISTORY OF COFFEE

Have you heard the story about the Ethiopian shepherd who discovered coffee? Supposedly he found his goats dancing with zeal around a coffee tree, having eaten some of the fruit that had fallen from it. It's a fun tale to tell, but it's more of a legend than a true origin story.

Coffee actually did originate in Ethiopia, where it grew wild, and Ethiopian tribes consumed it as early as the ninth century. But it wasn't until around the fifteenth century that traders from Yemen brought coffee beans back to the Middle East and began to cultivate them. The beverage soon became popular with monks, who found that it helped them concentrate during prayer. As the popularity of coffee increased, it spread throughout the Ottoman Empire.

As coffee made its way through Europe in the seventeenth century, it took root in London, where coffeehouses became a favorite location for men to socialize, discuss politics, and do business. As coffee culture spread throughout other European capitals, it took on a more cosmopolitan character. By the mid-eighteenth century, coffee had traveled around the world through various trade routes, including to the newly established United States.

Following the Boston Tea Party protests of 1773, various trade restrictions and boycotts of tea helped coffee become a permanent staple of American life. During this time in the mid-1700s, coffee farming had also spread. Emerging bean-growing industries in the Caribbean, India, and the Americas gave birth to a global industry of coffee cultivation, planting the seeds for coffee to transform U.S. culture (and, really, global culture) as we know it. From the early days of freeze-dried instant coffee to the foundation of modern cafés, coffee has become a ubiquitous American beverage that fuels our workers and unites us socially.

For most of its history, coffee has been treated like other generic commodities, such as corn or grain. Only in the past few decades has coffee been approached with quality in mind, leading to the rise of what we refer to today as "specialty coffee," the style that I focus on throughout this book. If you're a history buff, there are several books out there that dive much deeper into coffee's rich history (see "Resources," page 154), but for the purpose of brewing better coffee at home, know this: coffee is better now than it has ever been, and I want to help you enjoy it even more.

THE HISTORY OF COFFEE

850: According to legend, an Ethiopian shepherd watches as his goats get a boost of energy from eating coffee fruit.

1652: London's first coffee shop opens.

1686: Paris's first coffee shop opens.

1683: Vienna's first coffee shop opens, serving beans left behind by the Turkish army.

1900: Hills Bros. develop a vacuum-sealed tin for packing roasted coffee beans.

1903: German coffee importer Ludwig Roselius develops Sanka, the first commercial decaf.

1905: The first commercial espresso machine is made in Italy and sold by La Pavoni.

1933: Alfonso Bialetti invents the moka pot. Meanwhile, Dr. Ernest Illy invents the first automatic espresso machine.

1938: The Nestlé company introduces freeze-dried coffee as a solution for Brazil's coffee bean surplus. Soon after, Nescafé is introduced in Switzerland.

1942: During WWII, American soldiers are introduced to instant coffee in their meal kits. Back home in America, the government mandates a coffee ration.

1976: Nestlé researchers patent the first coffee pod.

2006: Specialty coffee accounts for about 40 percent of U.S. coffee sales.

Now: Coffee is the world's most popular beverage and one of its most traded commodities.

1400: Arab traders bring Ethiopian coffee beans to what is now Yemen, calling the brew *qahwa*, the Arab word for "wine."

1475: Ottoman Turks bring coffee to Constantinople, where it's brewed with spices, a style that continues today.

1607: Captain John Smith introduces coffee to the New World at the Jamestown settlement.

1727: Brazil's coffee industry launches after a coast guard officer smuggles seeds and cuttings into the country.

1773: Americans display their patriotism by switching to coffee after the Boston Tea Party.

1889: Hanson Goodrich patents the stovetop percolator.

1907: Brazil produces 97 percent of the world's coffee bean harvest.

1908: Melitta Bentz invents the drip coffee filter.

1920: Coffee sales boom after U.S. Prohibition kicks in.

1958: Juan Valdez, a fictional coffee grower, is introduced by the Colombian Coffee Federation.

1971: Starbucks opens its first location in Seattle, selling only fresh-roasted coffee beans.

1972: The Mr. Coffee machine is introduced by Ohio inventor Vincent Marotta.

THE BEAN

WHAT IS COFFEE?

The coffee bean is actually the seed of a fruit (the "cherry") that grows on a genus of flowering plants called *Coffea*. Usually referred to as trees, *Coffea* plants have wiry branches and large green leaves that, when left unmanaged, can grow fifteen feet tall or higher, but coffee farmers typically prune them to make it easier to harvest the cherries by hand.

SPECIES

There are roughly one hundred different species of *Coffea* trees, but only two of them are widely planted for their beans: arabica and canephora (commonly known as robusta). It's important to know which species you are purchasing because the differences between them relate to the quality and flavor of the coffee you drink. Arabica beans account for about 70 percent of the world's coffee production, and specialty coffees primarily use arabica beans because of their complex flavor profile. Arabica beans also require more care to farm and harvest, which makes them more expensive.

Robusta coffee, on the other hand, is generally considered by coffee professionals to be lower in quality than arabica. As the name "robusta" implies, trees of this species are more resistant to many diseases and are easier to grow and maintain. The hearty character of these beans and the large yields ultimately make them less expensive to produce and purchase. Robusta beans also have a higher caffeine content than arabica beans, and they are inherently bitter and have fewer subtle, pleasant flavors, which is why the majority of robusta beans are used in cheap, low-quality blends or instant coffee. Because you are reading this book, you are most likely buying and brewing arabica beans. If not, I suggest you spend the money to get the best possible coffee experience. You won't be disappointed!

VARIETY

Within the family of arabica coffee are numerous varieties, or subspecies. Some of the more common arabica varieties are Bourbon, Castillo, Caturra, Catuai, Geisha, Pacamara, SL28, SL34, and Typica, the first cultivated variety from which all others have descended. Some varieties, like the ones that come from Ethiopia, are heirloom, or naturally occurring, while others are hybrids developed to thrive in specific areas or environments or to be resistant to diseases that can plague coffee trees.

Just like the grapes used to make wine, each coffee variety contains different characteristics that determine the flavor profile of the final product. Likewise, the "terroir," or specific environmental conditions (including soil composition, altitude, and weather) where coffee trees grow, also affects the flavor of the beans. This means that the same bourbon coffee bean grown in Colombia will taste different from one grown in Rwanda because of environmental factors unique to each country.

Keep this wine analogy in mind when buying coffee beans. Just because you like a Cabernet from Napa Valley doesn't necessarily mean you'll like a Cabernet from France or Australia. Just like every bottle of wine, each coffee bean will be different, not only because of its variety and origin but also because of how it's handled and processed.

ANATOMY OF A COFFEE CHERRY

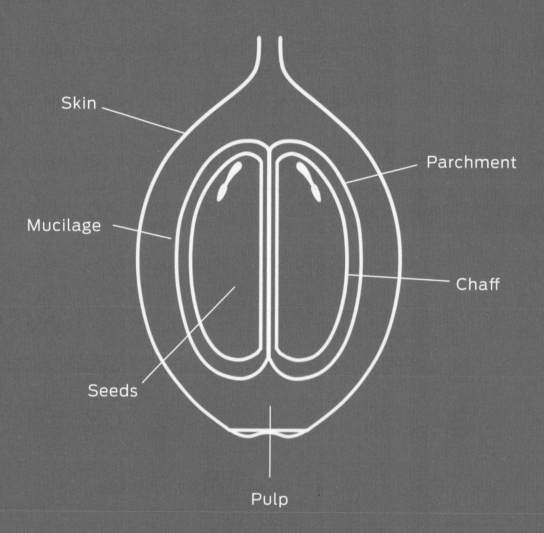

Skin

Parchment

Mucilage

Chaff

Seeds

Pulp

THE COFFEE CHERRY

Many coffee drinkers are surprised to learn that coffee beans come from a berry-like fruit. But it is precisely because of this origin that your coffee should remind you more of sweet fruit than bitter charcoal. Coffee seeds—the actual beans—commonly have one flat side and are nestled together as pairs inside the cherry. Peaberries are an exception. These genetic mutations result in only one smaller, unique round bean inside each cherry. Peaberries account for only about 5 percent of coffee beans, and growers sometimes sort them after processing to be sold as a unique coffee offering. Some people believe they are sweeter than regular beans, whereas others insist there's no difference. I think they can be quite delicious, but I don't usually seek them out.

The seeds are wrapped in a thin, silvery skin. This paper-like by-product, called "chaff," separates from the bean during roasting and is discarded or composted after. The silver-skinned seeds are wrapped in a thin, cream-colored shell referred to as "parchment." The parchment is covered in a sugary, gel-like substance known as the "mucilage," and a layer of fruit, which makes up the "pulp." A tight, colorful outer skin contains all of this.

Coffee cherries are edible straight from the tree, but there isn't a whole lot of fruit to be found between the skin and the seeds. They have a delicate flavor that is floral and lightly sweet like a melon, with a subtle, tart aftertaste.

THE COFFEE BELT

Coffee is grown in many parts of the world and is the primary export for at least a dozen countries. Most of the world's coffee farming occurs in developing countries located almost exclusively near the equator, between the Tropic of Cancer and the Tropic of Capricorn. These coffee-growing regions form a loop around the Earth's middle, which is why they are sometimes referred to as the "coffee belt." Coffee-producing countries along this belt include Mexico, Guatemala, Nicaragua, Honduras, El Salvador, Colombia, Costa Rica, Panama, Peru, Bolivia, and Brazil in the Americas; Uganda, Ethiopia, Kenya, Rwanda, Burundi, and Tanzania in Africa; and Thailand, Vietnam, and Indonesia in Asia.

It is from here that almost all of the world's commercially grown coffee originates. Though the lower cost of labor in these countries surely plays a role in the economics of growing coffee, the primary reason coffee is grown in the coffee belt is climate. Coffee grows best at higher altitudes with moderate temperatures and where there is a clear differentiation between rainy and dry seasons.

COFFEE FARMING

FARMING

A coffee tree begins as a seed in the nursery of a coffee farm. As the seedling grows, it's nurtured through several stages of development during its first year before being planted in the ground. The tree must grow another two to three years before it matures enough to provide a first harvest of coffee cherries. A single coffee tree yields only about one pound of coffee beans per year, which means that many coffee drinkers consume the entire annual harvest from a tree each week. As coffee trees get older, they produce fewer beans, so farmers plan ahead and strategize when to plant new trees, considering the three-year maturation period and how it will affect their total harvest and income in the the coming years. As long as a coffee tree is kept healthy, it can be productive for ten to twenty years before a new one needs to be replanted.

HARVESTING

As the cherries ripen, they turn from green to deep red (or yellow, in the case of some varieties), signaling that they're ready to be picked. Cherries also ripen at different rates, making harvesting a very labor-intensive process. Each tree often requires several picking passes as the fruit matures to prevent picking underripe coffee (which doesn't taste good) and reduce the amount of work needed to sort cherries by hand after they've been picked.

The harvest schedule for a coffee tree varies greatly depending on where it's grown, the altitude, how much rain the region receives, as well as the rainfall schedule. Most coffee-growing countries only have one annual harvest. But Colombia, for example, has one primary harvest and a smaller secondary har-

vest a few months later. After the coffee flowers blossom and are pollinated, it takes roughly six to nine months for the cherries to grow and ripen.

In most regions, coffee cherries are harvested by hand, although some larger farms use machines to shake cherries from their trees. The coffee cherries ripen at different times, so it takes pickers several passes over several months to harvest all of the coffee. The more focused on quality a farm is, the more attentive the farmer needs to be about when to pick the crop and the more it will cost to pay pickers to select and sort the best coffee cherries.

Sorting involves separating unripe and defective cherries from the good ones. This process can be done by hand or in tubs of water, wherein the unripe cherries float and the ripe cherries sink. It is just one of many steps in the harvesting process, but it is an incredibly important one that leads to the higher costs associated with specialty coffee. In many regions, coffee farms encompass less than a dozen acres of land, so the cherries are brought to a central-processing, or washing, station and mixed with those from nearby farms to create larger lots of roast-ready beans.

FARM TO CUP: A BEAN'S LIFE

Coffee tree planted

Cherries harvested

Processed: natural, washed, or honey

Hulled

Exported

Roasted

Bagged

Ground

Brewed

PROCESSING BEANS

Coffee processing includes all of the steps necessary to separate the coffee seeds (beans) from the rest of the cherry and results in a product that is ready to be roasted. The method used to process beans has a significant impact on a coffee's quality and flavor, like the fragrant blueberry notes of a natural-processed coffee from Ethiopia or the lively acidity of a washed coffee from Kenya.

Each coffee-producing region has its own bean-processing variations, which are usually determined by geographical characteristics, climate, and water availability. In some cases, a farmer may choose a particular processing method in order to achieve a desired flavor profile, making it a stylistic decision rather than an environmental one. Processing is one of the most complicated steps of a coffee bean's journey from the farm to your cup. But, as with bean varieties, when buying coffee it's only important to know the processing method if you have a particular preference.

There are three primary methods of coffee processing that you are likely to encounter while shopping for beans: natural, washed, and honey. The processing method is labeled on the bags of most specialty coffees, but large-scale commercial coffees rarely provide this kind of information (see page 34 for more about labels).

NATURAL PROCESSING
Coffee processed using the natural, or "sun-dried," method develops strong, fruity aromas and unique flavors derived from the cherry. This method leads to brewed coffee with a heavier body and a somewhat muted acidity. During natural processing, coffee cherries are laid out to dry in the sun. They must be routinely rotated with rakes so they don't over-

ferment, rot, and develop mold. It can take several weeks (depending on temperature and humidity) for the cherries to dry to the desired moisture level (around 10 to 12 percent) before they are milled to strip away the dried fruit and parchment surrounding the seeds, leaving them ready to be roasted.

Natural processing has developed a negative reputation among some coffee professionals who feel these coffees taste "dirty" or display notes of over-fermented fruit, but such flavors only develop when the cherries aren't processed with care. Some compare the flavors to those of natural wines in which nothing is added or taken away, leaving flavors that are more alive and even a bit funky. As someone who is more of a fan of natural wines than natural coffees, I disagree with this comparison (though it's worth mentioning for the sake of discussion.) While I find a glass of intensely flavored natural wine refreshing and enjoyable, a hot mug of naturally processed coffee is usually too pungent for my liking.

The natural method is the oldest and cheapest way to process beans, and though some farmers and coffee professionals consider it an inferior method, it is often a necessity in countries like Brazil and Ethiopia, where water is scarce. Recently, however, some farmers have made efforts to improve natural processing in order to produce beans that challenge some of the method's negative perceptions.

WASHED PROCESSING

Coffee processed using the washed method, also called "wet processing," develops clean and lively flavors that lead to more delicate nuances, an overall lighter body, and more pronounced acidity than that of the natural process. These characteristics are what make washed coffees the preferred style of many specialty coffee roasters.

During the washed method, coffee seeds are first "pulped," or squeezed from the cherry, by large, automatic machines or smaller hand-cranked ones. The leftover casings are thrown in compost piles to be used as fertilizer or can be dried and used for cascara, a caffeinated tea-like beverage that some specialty coffee roasters sell (see page 140). After being separated from the fruit, the seeds are still covered in sticky mucilage, so they are soaked in large tubs of water for twelve to seventy-two hours. This part of the process is referred to as "fermentation," wherein microbes feed on the sugary mucilage and remove it. The amount of fermentation time needed depends on different factors, such as temperature and the water quality, but it is important that seeds don't soak for too long or they can overferment, ruining the flavor.

After fermentation, the seeds are soaked again in clean water or rinsed before drying on patios, on raised beds, or in mechanical drying machines. Once the seeds have a moisture content of about 10 to 12 percent, which can take a couple weeks on patios or in beds or several hours in a machine. The coffee beans are then rested for up to two months before they are milled to remove the parchment, leaving behind green coffee beans ready to be exported and roasted.

HONEY PROCESSING

The honey method, also called "pulped natural" or "semiwashed," falls somewhere between washed and natural processing. Coffee cherries are pulped just as they are during washed processing, but instead of soaking in clean water, the beans are left to dry while still covered in the sticky mucilage. Once dried, the beans are rested for up to two months before they are milled (to remove the parchment) and ready to be shipped.

This method of processing can be used by farmers for environmental (water restrictions) or stylistic (to achieve specific flavor profiles) reasons. When done well, honey processing results in cleaner-tasting coffee with an acidity similar to the washed-processing method, while maintaining some of the pungent aromas and complex fruitiness that make natural-processed beans so unique. Given the choice, I usually prefer a honey-processed to a natural-processed coffee precisely for its balance of characteristics that I enjoy the most.

THE ETHICS OF COFFEE

It's no secret that coffee beans are primarily grown in developing countries, and it is precisely because of this that a cup of coffee—including the relatively more expensive specialty coffee—can be so cheap. However, growing and harvesting coffee is very labor intensive, with very few ways to automate the process, and the best coffees can cost more to produce because of the extra steps and increased labor required.

The beans used to make your coffee have been touched by dozens of hands and traveled thousands of miles before being brewed and poured into your mug, but you still only pay about half of what it costs to buy a bottle of craft beer or a glass of wine out on the town. These price discrepancies create real issues along the coffee supply chain and are beginning to raise concerns about the long-term sustainability of the specialty coffee market. Hopefully a better understanding of this reality will lead to a better appreciation of your daily cup of coffee, because you are still getting a great deal in the relative scope of small luxuries.

How can you tell if the coffee you buy is ethical? Some people rely heavily on Fair Trade and organic certification to guide them, but these labels only tell you so much. The prices paid to farmers for their Fair Trade–certified coffee are still based on the global commodities market, and the prices set by this market have no correlation to how good the coffee tastes. There are also barriers to becoming certified Fair Trade or organic that can prevent smaller farmers from participating.

Although most green (unroasted) coffee is sold through the global commodities market at a fairly low and volatile price, specialty coffee is sold through personal agreements based more specifically on quality and flavor, including a coffee's "cupping score" (see page 72 for more on cupping). Many specialty coffee roasters, whether buying directly from farmers or with the help of coffee importers, pay premium prices for their green coffee beans based on the quality of the product rather than the whims of global trading markets. The prices paid to farmers for specialty coffee is often much higher than even Fair Trade, further complicating what it means to buy ethically. When it's in the interest of specialty coffee roasters to find the best beans, they are willing to pay more as long as there is a market to support it. This means that the better the coffee, the more money a farmer is able get for it and the more incentive there is to continue improving. However, all of this requires that consumers are willing to pay more for beans as well.

The challenge with the specialty coffee model is that there are no universal certifications or regulations to guide you when purchasing coffee beans, and marketing can be misleading. Some brands purporting to sell high-quality coffee beans are doing little more than dressing up inferior beans with slick packaging and marketing. The best way to truly know where your coffee comes from and how it was purchased is to find a local roaster and ask. If your local coffee roaster is buying quality coffee (you will hopefully be able to taste the difference), he or she will be more than happy to tell you all about it.

SPECIALTY COFFEE

Throughout this book I primarily refer to "specialty coffee," which is essentially coffee that is produced with the highest quality and best flavors in mind. Ultimately, it is more "special" than low-grade commodity coffee, which is produced with no real consideration other than that it is coffee. The coffee beans that are good enough to be described as "specialty" come from specific countries or regions, can be identified by their unique flavors, and meet a standard set by the coffee industry itself. Within the coffee industry, there is a one-hundred-point scoring system that professionals use to evaluate a coffee according to many factors, including flavor, aroma, sweetness, acidity, and whether it has defects or not. When a coffee receives more than eighty points on this scale, it is technically considered specialty coffee. However, it is important to note that within that twenty-point window there is still a broad range of quality. Specialty coffee includes everything from that which is produced by big coffee shop chains like Starbucks to the small uncompromising coffee roasters who search for only exceptional coffee beans and strive to produce the best flavors possible. It's these small roasters who are committed to discovering the exceptional quality and flavors that I love. These are the coffees that I refer to when I mention "specialty."

DECAFFEINATED COFFEE

Many people don't know this, but decaffeinated coffee doesn't come from a specific kind of bean; it's the result of a process that removes most (at least 97 percent) of the caffeine content from any unroasted coffee bean. Various methods are used to remove caffeine from coffee, but they generally involve minor variations to a similar approach.

CHEMICAL DECAFFEINATION

This method begins with green coffee beans either steamed or soaked in water to open up the pores before being rinsed several times with chemicals such as methylene chloride or ethyl acetate that extract the caffeine. Sometimes the beans are soaked in a coffee extract afterward that is meant to reintroduce the flavors and oils that the process strips away.

SWISS WATER DECAFFEINATION

The chemical-free Swiss Water approach uses a charcoal filter to remove caffeine after the green beans are soaked in very hot water. The beans are then bathed in a green-coffee extract to reintroduce some of the flavors lost during the initial stages of the process.

Many coffee producers, sellers, and consumers recognize Swiss Water as a superior and more eco-friendly way to remove caffeine, and some brands that employ it advertise its use, but even still, decaf can sometimes be hard to find in specialty coffee cafés. If you drink decaffeinated coffee—either by choice or by necessity—you may feel that your needs have been ignored, but it's not (usually) out of spite. As far as one's palate is concerned, decaffeinated coffee is underwhelming compared to regular coffee because so much of the flavor is stripped away during the decaffeination process.

Because there are extra costs associated with removing caffeine from coffee beans, and since much of the flavor is diminished, lesser-quality beans are often used to lower the final price.

Speaking from personal experience, customers who order decaf coffee at a specialty coffee shop make up a small percentage of sales, so it's not worth the expense or counter space for most shops to carry and brew decaf when tastier and more popular noncaffeinated options, such as tea or juice, can be made available. As inconvenient as this may be for caffeine-averse customers, to not roast or sell decaffeinated coffee is usually a business decision (and not a personal one). That said, any establishment that shames you for eschewing caffeine doesn't deserve your business.

ROASTING

One of the most important and impactful steps of the coffee process is transforming raw, green coffee beans into the roasted ones we brew. The primary goal of roasting coffee is to develop aromas and flavors by quickly heating green beans until several chemical reactions take place, including pyrolysis, the Maillard reaction, and caramelization, which develop the sugars and acids in the beans. Similar reactions occur when you bake bread or cookies to produce the delicious flavors that we enjoy.

Roasting styles vary broadly from company to company, and each roaster has his or her own opinion about the best methods. Most commercial roasting is accomplished with drum roasters, which range in size depending on the volume a roaster wants to process. Some machines roast only a few pounds at a time, whereas others can handle hundreds of pounds of beans. Drum roasters tumble the coffee beans around, much like a clothes dryer, while a combination of convection and conduction heat the beans. The entire process, from when the green beans are first poured into the roaster to when they drop into a cooling tray, varies according to the roaster's desired style and roast level, but generally it takes ten to fifteen minutes. Temperatures in the roaster can reach 450°F by the time roasting is complete, and they fluctuate constantly during the process. A key part of successful coffee roasting is being able to monitor and manage these changes in temperature over time. Once a roaster loses control of these variables, the consistency and quality of each roast is at risk.

Near the end of the roasting process, when the flavors begin to develop, gases that have built up in the coffee beans expand very quickly, causing an audible cracking sound as they escape the beans. This "first crack," as it is called, happens at around 380°F, and it is an important indicator of progress for the roaster. Most light- to medium-roast beans are finished shortly after this crack. If a darker roast is the goal, the temperature will continue to rise and the beans will experience a "second crack" at around 435°F. Most specialty coffee roasters stop before the second crack. Roasting up to and beyond the second crack is reserved for much darker styles of coffee, in which the flavors of the roast itself replace the flavors of the coffee (see "Roast Levels" on page 30 for more information).

Once the beans have been roasted to the desired level, a door at the bottom of the roaster drum is opened and the beans drop onto a large cooling tray. A set of slowly spinning blades stir the beans, cooling them down quickly to stop the roasting process. Once the beans have cooled, they are packed into airtight bags and shipped to customers.

ROASTING COFFEE AT HOME

While it's possible to buy green coffee beans and roast them in your own kitchen, it's not something I recommend. Roasting beans isn't very difficult, but the results will never compare to what experienced professionals accomplish using very accurate roasters that costs tens of thousands of dollars. If you're curious about DIY roasting, however, there are online forums dedicated to highly passionate people who use everything from ovens to modified popcorn poppers to miniature home-roasting

machines to roast beans at home. Hobby roasters truly enjoy the process and the satisfaction of being in charge of their beans, but results may vary.

ROAST LEVELS

Understanding the roast level or color of coffee beans can help you determine if a particular coffee meets your personal flavor preferences, but describing the roast level of a bean is an ambiguous task. There are many stylistic names used to describe roast levels, including "city roast," "full city roast," "French roast," and "Italian roast." However, all of these names are nebulous at best and mean different things to different roasters around the world. These terms are fairly outdated, but you may still find them listed on coffee bags at the grocery store; it's rare to see any of them used by specialty coffee roasters, with the exception of larger chains such as Starbucks that still find marketing value in the terms.

Since choosing a roast level ultimately depends on personal taste, there is no "best" or "worst" level. Just as some folks like their steaks rare, others prefer them well-done. However, if you find yourself at a world-class restaurant, it's often best to rely on the chef's expertise to cook the meat to a degree that yields the best flavor. Similarly, specialty coffee roasters pride themselves on identifying which roast level highlights the best flavors of a specific bean, and they do this by developing what is called a "roast profile." Rather than relying on ambiguous color designations, they describe each individual coffee they make by the flavors brought out during the roasting process.

For simplicity, in this book I separate roast levels into three categories: light, medium, and dark (just remember that within each category exists a broad range of levels). Most of the roast profiles used for specialty coffee fall on the light to medium side of the scale and are ideal for the brewing methods covered later in this book. In this range, the roaster's intention is to highlight the coffee's inherent complexity and coax out the delicate flavors that reflect how the beans were grown and processed. When roasted well, these coffees are naturally sweet with distinguishable flavors that range from fruits to chocolate to nuts, and they have a balanced acidity.

Medium- to dark-roast beans are often intended for espresso because they have less acidity and more body, which favor that brewing method. If roasted for too long, dark-roast coffee tastes unpleasant and retains very little of the coffee beans' inherent flavors. Italian-style blends and French and Vienna roasts are on the darkest end of the spectrum. These dark coffees derive their flavor from the longer roasting process itself, leading to a coffee that tastes like smoke, ash, and carbon and is bitter and astringent. Roasters may intentionally roast coffee beans this dark because of the roaster's preference, to mask lower-quality beans, or to create a uniform dark-roast flavor that has a longer shelf life and a large base of customers who are accustomed to drinking it.

COFFEE ROAST COLOR SPECTRUM

Use these color descriptions to help you identify various roast levels.

Unroasted: pale greenish-grey

Drying Phase: yellow or tan (before first crack)

Light Roast: matte brown, similar to the color of milk chocolate (just after first crack)

Medium Roast: matte brown, slightly darker than the color of milk chocolate

Dark Roast: dark-chocolate brown, with some oily specks (around second crack)

Burnt: dark brown or black in color, glossy from oil (after second crack)

SINGLE ORIGIN VS BLENDED

Coffee beans can be packaged and sold as single-origin or a blend. Neither approach is inherently better; they are simply different ways to enjoy coffee. While single-origin coffee is a direct reflection of how an individual bean tastes, a blend is meant to showcase a specific flavor profile created by the roaster. Just as some Scotch enthusiasts prefer single-malt whiskey to a blended one (or vice versa), some coffee drinkers prefer single-origin coffees over blends.

SINGLE-ORIGIN COFFEE

Using single-origin coffee is the purist approach to enjoying your daily brew (and personally what I like to use to prepare mine). A single-origin coffee is identified by the geographic region it comes from, but the specificity of that origin can vary. A single-origin coffee can simply acknowledge the country where it was grown, or it can more narrowly specify a region of a country, the processing station, the farm, and even a specific lot number. Every coffee-producing country has different conventions for determining and naming origins, but the more transparent and specific a roaster can be when identifying a single-origin coffee, the better it is for consumer awareness. Apart from the transparency regarding where a specific coffee came from, many people enjoy single-origin coffee for its flavor diversity. Coffee is an incredibly complex beverage, and most coffee enthusiasts want to identify and enjoy the nuances of flavor that come from a specific bean variety and its terroir. Once again, it helps to compare coffee and wine: while it can be nice to drink a red blend made from grapes sourced from many locations, others find it more illuminating to explore a single-varietal wine from a specific vineyard.

BLENDED COFFEE

It's assumed that people who prefer single-origin coffees believe blends are inferior, but there are great blends made with high-quality beans and delicious intent. Because coffee beans are a seasonal product, the availability of certain single-origin beans varies throughout the year (and from year to year). One of the main reasons roasters blend beans is so they can produce a coffee with a consistent flavor profile year-round. When done well, a bean blend creates a balanced-tasting brew that many coffee drinkers prefer over that of single-origin beans.

Specialty coffee companies usually include a blend or two in their lineup because they're approachable for many people, which often makes them best sellers. It's very common for a coffee shop to offer an everyday blend for drip coffee and to use a blend for espresso, which balances out the acidity that an espresso machine can amplify.

The way blends are created depends on the style of the roaster and the type of beans being used. However, there are many roasters who use blends for purely economic reasons, cutting costs by adding low-quality beans into the mix. Some coffee brands (especially those that deal with Italian-style roasts) mix cheaper robusta coffee beans into their products, which adds extra caffeine along with an unpleasant bitterness.

BUYING COFFEE

When buying coffee beans, think of them as perishable produce rather than a pantry staple that can be stored indefinitely. Even though coffee will not spoil in the same way that fresh produce will, its flavors are quite volatile and start breaking down soon after the roasting process. The aromatics that provide the complex flavors diminish over time until the beans taste stale and lifeless. Old coffee beans won't harm you, but they won't have nearly as much flavor as when they were fresh. Most coffee is at its best for two to three weeks after roasting, which is why I recommend buying coffee in smaller amounts that can be consumed in that range of time.

However, it's also possible to have coffee that is *too* fresh. Freshly roasted beans expel lots of gases, including carbon dioxide, that are a result of the roasting process. This period, known as "degassing," is at its most extreme during the first few post-roast days, and those gases can have a negative effect on how coffee tastes. Degassing is why some coffee bags have little plastic valves on them, which allow the gases to escape while keeping the coffee beans protected from oxygen, the main culprit that degrades beans. Brewing beans that have come directly from the roaster isn't bad for you, per se, but the beans won't taste their best until they've had a chance to rest and degas for a couple of days.

Buy your coffee beans directly from a local roaster or coffee shop whenever possible. If this isn't an option, visit a higher-end grocery store that features local specialty coffee roasters. If you live in a community that doesn't have a good, local coffee roaster, there are a number of great sources for buying specialty beans online (see "Resources," page 154). Companies such as MistoBox offer customized coffee bean subscriptions, and most specialty coffee roasters will ship their coffee anywhere. If you currently buy your coffee from a supermarket chain, I suggest changing your routine. The coffee section at the typical grocery store rarely includes specialty coffee, and you'll be hard-pressed to find beans that list a roast date, which means their freshness is highly questionable. Always look for a roast date when buying coffee; ideally the beans will have been roasted within the last week.

READING THE PACKAGE

If you're new to buying specialty coffee, you'll probably see a lot of information on the bag that you haven't encountered before. Ultimately it's up to each roaster to decide what and how much information to share, but there are several common details that you're likely to find:

Region of origin (the country where it was grown, or a more specific locale)

Name of the farm, co-op, and/or wet mill (where the bean was grown and/or processed)

Bean variety(ies)

Altitude (beans grown at higher altitudes are often more acidic and complex)

Roasting date (If it doesn't have a roasting date, beware!)

Flavor profile (a description of how your coffee will taste, when brewed properly)

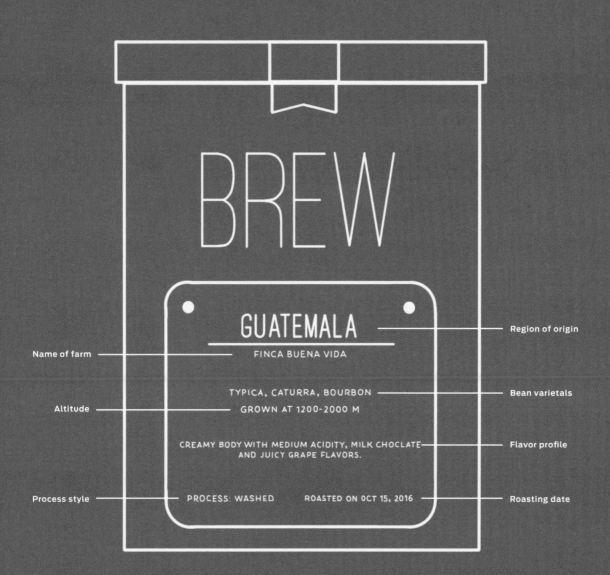

BREW

Name of farm

Altitude

Process style

GUATEMALA
FINCA BUENA VIDA

TYPICA, CATURRA, BOURBON
GROWN AT 1200-2000 M

CREAMY BODY WITH MEDIUM ACIDITY, MILK CHOCLATE
AND JUICY GRAPE FLAVORS.

PROCESS: WASHED   ROASTED ON OCT 15, 2016

Region of origin

Bean varietals

Flavor profile

Roasting date

STORING BEANS

The best way to preserve the freshness and flavor of coffee beans is to store them in an airtight container away from moisture, sunlight, oxygen, and heat. Many coffee roasters sell their beans in resealable packaging that works well to maintain freshness, but placing the beans in an airtight storage container adds another level of protection from the elements that degrade their delicate flavors.

Despite the many myths you've likely heard about storing beans in the refrigerator and freezer to prolong freshness, I recommend against this practice (unless they're vacuum sealed for longer-term storage). When coffee beans are chilled and then rewarmed, condensation forms on the beans and speeds up the degradation process. Besides the damage done by moisture, beans stored in the refrigerator or freezer can absorb the aromas and flavors of other foods as well.

I've said it before, but I'll say it again: the best path to fresh coffee is to buy fresh beans and only the amount you'll consume within a week or two. However, properly stored beans can retain their flavor for up to two months, though you may find the flavors of the brewed coffee muted. Coffee beans don't look or smell a certain way when they get old, but the aroma of the beans, just like their flavor, will fade with time. Dark-roast beans might seem to hold up longer because most of their flavor is derived from the roasting process itself. This is one reason why the packages of commercial dark-roast beans don't usually list roast dates. If you have no clue how old those beans are that you found in the back of your cupboard, rest assured that the coffee you brew with them won't harm you—it probably just won't taste very good.

THE TOOLS

GRINDERS

Of all the ways to improve brewing coffee at home, having a good burr grinder is one of the greatest investments you can make. It will take your coffee brewing to a completely new level of deliciousness. If you brew coffee every day, you should invest in a good grinder—I guarantee it will be used more often and bring more joy to your countertop than any other appliance. When shopping for a coffee grinder, it's important to know the two common types of grinders and why one style is far superior to the other (answer: uniformity).

Burr grinders use a set of burrs to turn coffee beans into smaller grounds. The burrs can be oriented either as a set of two nesting cones with vertical ridges or a set of flat, circular plates with radial ridges; they are made from either ceramic or metal. A burr grinder produces a uniform grind because of how the burrs crush and squeeze the beans through a defined space rather than chopping them into pieces. The amount of space between the two burrs determines the grind size, and it can be adjusted to accommodate various brewing methods. During grinding, the beans pass from a storage chamber down through the spinning burrs and the coffee grounds collect in a container below. The price of a burr grinder can range from about $30 for a manual, hand-operated grinder to $300 for a fancier motorized one. Price doesn't always reflect quality with grinders; you can find several hand grinders made by companies such as Porlex and Hario that produce better grind quality and cost less than some cheaper electric grinders. However, even the cheapest burr grinder is preferable to buying preground coffee or using a blade grinder.

Blade grinders use a spinning blade, much like a blender, to shatter and splinter coffee beans into particles that range in size from powdery dust to large chunks. A blade grinder has one chamber with a spinning blade and a button that turns the machine on and off. The longer the blade turns, the finer, or smaller, the coffee grounds are supposed to get. However, there's no way to set a desired grind size, and the operator has very little control over the final outcome of the coffee grounds. (One way to get slightly better uniformity is to gently shake the grinder while the blade is spinning.) Blade grinders are still, unfortunately, more popular than burr grinders, and many of you likely have one in your kitchen. Manufacturers often refer to them as "spice grinders," and they should be reserved for just that. The big difference between a good burr grinder and a cheap blade grinder is how well they actually create uniform coffee grounds, which is vital for getting proper and consistent flavor extraction when brewing.

SCALES

As I explain in the "Measuring" section (see page 66), a digital kitchen scale is an essential tool for brewing coffee in an accurate and consistent way. Just as every good baker should use a scale, so should anyone who brews a lot of coffee at home. Digital scales vary widely in price and features, from $10 for a basic one to $150 or more for a scale specifically designed for coffee. You don't need anything more than a basic digital scale as long as it has a few essential features. You want one that measures at least to the tenth of a gram (0.1) and can weigh at least 5 pounds of beans and gear. It's also important to find a scale large enough to hold whatever equipment you use to brew your coffee, and one that doesn't automatically turn off too quickly to avoid a shutdown while brewing. A built-in timer is also convenient, but most extra features are luxuries that you don't need.

START
STOP

00'00" 00.0 g

ON/OFF
TARE

KETTLES

While a standard water kettle will work for most of the brewing methods I discuss in this book, a special gooseneck kettle can make pour-over coffee a much easier endeavor. When brewing pour-over coffee, it's important to control the stream of water so you can saturate the coffee grounds at a slow and steady rate. Gooseneck kettles are designed specifically for this task, and many manufacturers make them. What makes a gooseneck kettle stand out from a basic kettle is how balanced it feels in your hand and how slowly and controlled the water pours from the tip of the spout. A gooseneck kettle is not a requirement for making pour-over coffee, but it can add to the experience and the consistency of your brewing efforts. However, if I were prioritizing my coffee equipment purchases, I recommend getting a scale first.

POUR-OVER DRIPPERS

Drip coffee is one of the most common ways to brew coffee at home in the United States. In the simplest of terms, this method involves pouring hot water over a cone that holds a filter with coffee grounds in it. Gravity pulls water through the coffee, which passes through the filter and is funneled by the cone into a vessel below. Coffee can be brewed this way using an electric drip brewer, which are manufactured by numerous companies in countless variations, or by using a manual pour-over dripper, which I focus on in this book.

Pour-over drippers come in a variety of shapes and sizes and are made of different materials. All drippers accomplish the same task in a similar way, with slight variations. The primary differences are the type of filters that they use and the size of the hole in the bottom of the cone, which determines how quickly water can pass through the grounds. Fans of each type will argue why their favorite is the best one to use. Ultimately, it's possible to make delicious coffee with each type of dripper as long as you understand some basics for brewing better coffee.

The **Chemex** is an hourglass-shaped glass carafe that doubles as the coffee brewer and vessel. Created by Dr. Peter Schlumbohm, the Chemex is a design icon that has found a home in the permanent collection at the MoMA and on countertops around the world. The proprietary filters are made from a thick, bonded paper. The Chemex brews a very bright and clean cup of coffee; however, it is prone to clogging and overextracting, which makes it unpopular with some people. The Chemex is made in the United States and comes in several sizes.

The **Hario V60** is a circular cone with a single dime-sized hole at the bottom that allows water to flow through the coffee grounds relatively unrestricted compared to other drippers. The V60 derives its name from the 60-degree angle of its walls. The inside walls of the V60 have radial ridges that aid the flow of water. You can only purchase its filters in specialty shops or online. Made in Japan, the V60 comes in three sizes and is made of ceramic, glass, plastic, or stainless steel.

The **Kalita Wave** is a circular, flat-bottomed cone with horizontal ridges and three small holes in the bottom. The small holes restrict the water flow more than a V60 or a Chemex and are meant to produce more consistent extraction, brew after brew. The flat-bottomed filters resemble those used with standard electric drip brewers, but they must be purchased at specialty shops or online. The filter has vertical pleats that help retain heat and keep the water flowing through the coffee. Made in Japan, the Kalita Wave comes in two sizes and is made of ceramic, glass, or stainless steel.

The **Melitta** is a circular cone that tapers into a linear wedge with one to three small holes in the bottom, which restrict the flow of the water and help create a more consistent extraction from brew to brew. Vertical ridges line the walls and aid the flow of water. One of the benefits of the Melitta is that its paper filters are readily available and can be purchased at most supermarkets. Invented by Melitta Bentz in Germany, the Melitta dripper comes in several sizes and is made of ceramic or plastic.

ELECTRIC DRIP

Electric drip machines are ubiquitous in many homes and probably one of the more common methods that people use to brew coffee. Electric drip machines brew coffee in a similar way to the pour-over method, the primary difference being that the coffeemaker heats and pours the water. The problem with most of these brewers is twofold: most of the time the heating elements aren't very good, so the water temperature is not hot or consistent enough for good extraction, and the water is sprayed haphazardly over the grounds without thorough or balanced saturation.

There are a few high-quality electric drip machines on the market from brands such as Moccamaster, Wilfa, Bonavita, and Ratio, and other manufacturers plan to offer more and better options in the future. If you like this style of coffeemaker, the important thing to look for when shopping for one is a seal of approval from the Specialty Coffee Association (SCA). SCA certification means that the machine in question has passed specifications for proper water temperature and saturation of the coffee grounds. I also recommend choosing a machine with a thermal carafe instead of a hot plate. Hot plates will overheat the coffee, leading to unwanted flavors.

DRIP FILTERS

While it's common to associate drip coffee with paper filters, there are several different materials used for filters that can affect the texture and flavor of your drip coffee, and some also provide reusable options for those who want to reduce waste.

CLOTH

Cloth filters are commonly used with a pour-over method known as the "nel drip" or "woodneck," a method used in Japan and parts of South America in which coffee is brewed through a sock-like sack. But cloth filters can also be found for most pour-over drippers. Like paper filters, cloth filters capture much of the sediment, but they allow more of the coffee oils to pass into the cup. This adds more body and texture than coffee brewed with a paper filter, while also muting the acidity. Many people use cloth filters because they are reusable, but cleaning and storing them properly requires extra effort, which turns most people away from them.

PAPER

Paper filters are the most common type of filter used for drip brewing. Paper produces the smoothest coffee texture with the least amount of sediment and, compared to other filters, prevents the most coffee oils from passing into the cup. You can purchase white or "natural" brown paper filters; however, the natural ones can affect the taste of your coffee much more than the white ones. (People tend to think that white filters are worse for the environment, but these days they are whitened using oxygen instead of harsh bleaching chemicals.) When you are finished brewing, used paper filters can be easily composted along with the coffee grounds, making cleanup relatively easy without much of an environmental burden.

METAL

Metal filters are standard with the French press and moka pot, but you can also find versions for various drip-coffee methods and the AeroPress. Metal filters allow the most sediment and coffee oils to pass into the cup, which results in a coffee with more body and texture. Some people really enjoy these characteristics in their coffee, while others prefer the clarity of a paper or cloth filter. Metal filters are long-lasting and reusable, but they need to be kept clean.

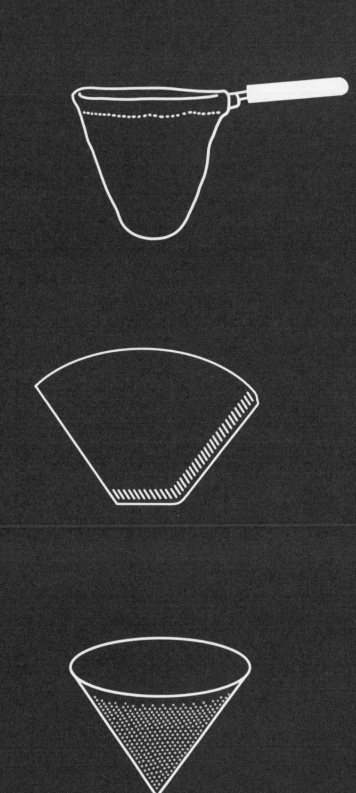

FRENCH PRESS

The French press, also known as a "press pot" or "cafetière," is a very common method of immersion brewing in which the grounds are steeped in hot water like tea. I highly recommend this method to anyone who is new to brewing coffee for themselves because French presses are incredibly easy to use. You can buy one made of glass, stainless steel, or ceramic, but the main difference between these materials is ruggedness and how well they insulate the coffee. Nearly every French press uses the same type of mesh filter with little variation between brands. The one exception is the Espro Press, which has a dual filter that reduces the amount of sediment in the coffee.

The coffee grounds steep in hot water in the pot for several minutes before you push down a metal rod with a filter on the end, trapping the coffee grounds at the base of the unit and filtering the liquid. A cup of coffee brewed with a French press is quite similar to that brewed during a cupping (see page 72). The French press is also a good method for tasting the flavors of a coffee with all of its oils intact. Coffee from a French press will also have more body than that of brew methods using a paper filter because the coffee oils and sediment are allowed to pass through the mesh. If you enjoy a little more texture in your coffee, the French press might be your ideal brewing method.

AEROPRESS

The AeroPress is a unique and versatile brewing device that is relatively new to the world of coffee. Invented in 2005 by Alan Adler (who also created the Aerobie flying disc), it has acquired a bit of a cult following, including a coffee-brewing World Championship dedicated solely to the AeroPress.

This hybrid brewing device combines immersion brewing and pressure brewing to deliver the clean body of a drip coffee passed through a paper filter. The AeroPress is similar to a French press in that coffee grounds are steeped with water for a set amount of time. However, the pressure used to force the coffee through the device reduces the overall brewing time. The device works like a large syringe, only instead of a needle on the bottom there is a porous cap that holds the paper filter in place. The coffee steeps in the bottom half of the AeroPress before the top half is used to plunge the liquid through the filter, injecting the coffee into a vessel. Part of the device's popularity among coffee enthusiasts is its flexibility; variations on how to use the AeroPress include making a strong concentrate that can be diluted with hot water or simply brewing a single cup that resembles drip coffee. AeroPress enthusiasts have come up with countless other brewing techniques and recipes, making it something like an open-source coffeemaker. Its small size and nearly unbreakable structure also make it ideal for traveling. I pack one along with a small hand-crank grinder on almost every trip I take.

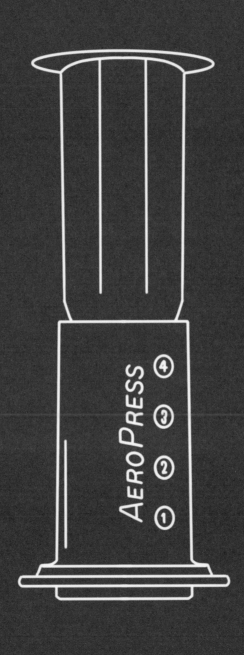

MOKA POT

The Bialetti Moka Express, named after its creator, Alfonso Bialetti, is known to many people as the stovetop espresso maker or "moka pot." While it doesn't actually make true espresso, it does use steam pressure to produce a strong, syrupy style of coffee that espresso drinkers often prefer over drip coffee. The moka pot is one of the most iconic of all home-brewing devices due to its unique design, and it's said to be so popular among Italians that you can find one in nine out of ten kitchens in Italy. These coffee brewers are self-contained and only require a heat source to work, but I find them rather complicated. The only reason I'm including this method in the book is because moka pots are ubiquitous, and I hope my tips (see page 86) can help improve the coffee made by those determined to use it. It can be difficult to control the extraction of the coffee with a moka pot, and I find the resulting brew bitter and metallic tasting. Some people also say that you shouldn't clean your moka pot so that it becomes "seasoned," like a cast-iron skillet, but I highly recommend keeping your coffee-brewing equipment clean to prevent rancid coffee oils from tainting the taste of fresh coffee.

THE BREW

EXTRACTION

While many people say that making coffee is an art, it's mostly just simple science. At its most basic, brewed coffee is the combination of time, water, and, of course, ground beans. But if you want your coffee to taste delicious every time you brew a cup, it is important to learn how to control the variables that affect taste and identify when one of them is off. The variables that impact coffee brewing the most are the size of the coffee grounds (grind size), how much coffee and water is used (dose/ratio), and how long the water is in contact with the coffee (brew time). Once you learn how to monitor and adjust these variables, you'll be able to brew great coffee every time.

The process of drawing flavors out of coffee grounds and into water is called "extraction," and it determines how good your coffee tastes. While coffee grounds can't completely dissolve in water—instant coffee is another matter—there's a sweet spot with every brew in which the right amount of flavor (and the right flavors) is extracted from the grounds and dissolved in the water (see the chart on page 69).

When coffee is "underextracted," it means the water did not spend enough time in contact with the grounds, and too little of the flavor was removed. An underextracted coffee can taste weak, sour, and salty. When coffee is "overextracted," it means the water and coffee grounds spent too much time in contact with each other and too much flavor was removed from the beans, including bad-tasting chemical compounds. An overextracted cup of coffee can taste strong, bitter, and astringent. A coffee that is properly extracted will taste smooth, balanced, and naturally sweet. There will be a nice clarity in the flavors and a pleasant lingering finish.

TIME

The amount of time that water is in contact with the coffee grounds plays an important role in determining how much of the coffee flavors are extracted. Too little time and the coffee will be underextracted and sour. Too much time and it will be overextracted and bitter. As little as fifteen to thirty seconds either way can dramatically affect the extraction and flavor of your coffee; this is why monitoring and controlling brew time is so important to the final result. How you control extraction time will depend on what method you use to brew coffee, but you can easily keep track of the time with a kitchen timer or a cell phone.

When brewing drip coffee (which includes pour-over and electric drip machines), the primary way to control the extraction time of the brew is to adjust the grind size. If your coffee is underextracted and you want the water to spend more time in contact with the coffee, grind the coffee finer. A smaller grind size forces water to pass more slowly through the grounds, increasing the time they are in contact. Conversely, if the coffee is overextracted, then a coarser grind will allow water to pass through the grounds more quickly, decreasing the time the water is in contact with the coffee. You can experiment with the grind size to find out what makes the coffee taste the way you enjoy it the most. The same rules apply for pressure-based brewing methods, such as the moka pot or AeroPress: a finer grind slows the water down as it's forced through the grounds, and a coarser grind will speed the process up.

When using an immersion brewing method, such as the French press or AeroPress, it's easier to control brew time and extraction without changing grind size: simply adjust the amount of time that passes before you push the plunger down. However, you can still work with various grind sizes to achieve the desired results, keeping in mind that a finer grind needs less time to hit the extraction sweet spot than a coarser grind. As with the other brewing methods, experiment until you find the amount of time and grind size that works best for you (see "Grinding," page 70).

WATER

A cup of coffee is roughly 98 percent water, which means that the water used to brew your coffee has a significant impact on how the coffee tastes. Many specialty coffee shops use expensive water-treatment systems to filter water and dial in a specific mineral and pH balance. Your options are more limited when brewing coffee at home, but here's what you need to know: you should use water that doesn't have unwanted odors or flavors (like chlorine) but contains enough mineral content for good extraction. Distilled water is devoid of minerals, which are essential for flavor extraction, and should be avoided.

An experience I had in London helped me realize how much water affects the flavor of coffee. I was taking part in a comparative coffee tasting in which a dozen different coffees were on the table. One of the samples was a cheap, preground coffee from the grocery store, and the others were a range of high-quality specialty coffees. At the end of the table, one of the specialty coffees was featured twice—one brewed using London tap water and the other with treated water. The difference between the two was like night and day. The specialty coffee brewed with tap water tasted nearly as bad as the cheap, preground coffee, and the water used to make it was the culprit.

Depending on where you live and how your water is treated, the quality of your tap water may be fine. But if you don't like the flavor of your tap water, a pitcher-based water filter can improve it. If it still has an "off" flavor after filtering, experiment with different bottled waters. Each brand will affect the flavor of the coffee, but some favorites among coffee enthusiasts include Evian, Voss, and Volvic.

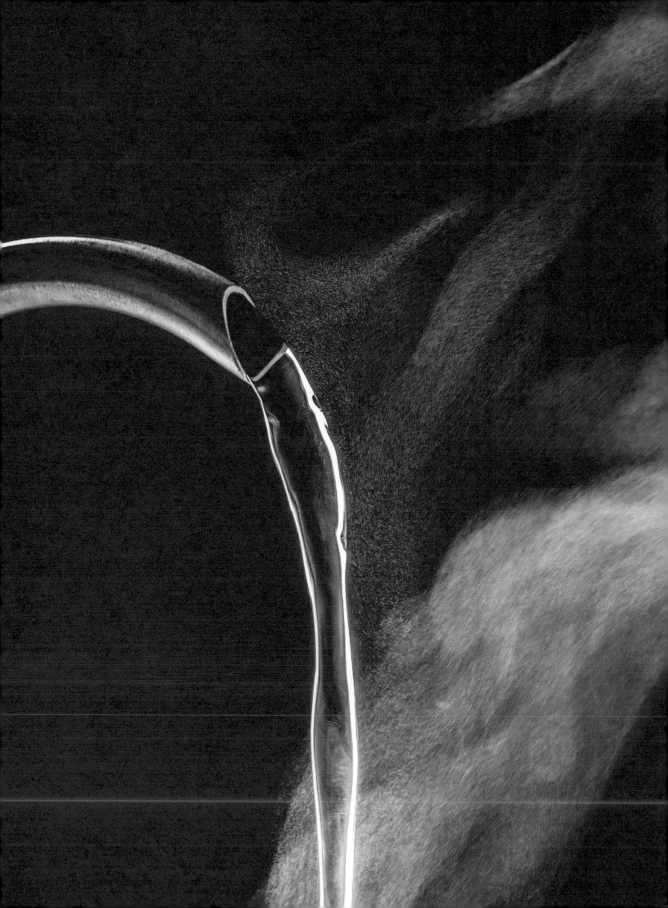

TEMPERATURE

The temperature of the water used for brewing coffee also plays an important role in extraction. If the water is not hot enough, it can't extract all of the complex flavors that make a cup of coffee so delicious (this also holds true to cold-brew coffee; see page 92). One of the reasons why most electric drip machines are so bad at making coffee is that the water doesn't get (or stay) hot enough through the entire brewing cycle.

On the other hand, water that's too hot can extract bitter flavors that you don't want in your coffee. The ideal temperature for brewing coffee is between 200ºF and 205ºF. If you don't have an instant-read thermometer, wait about two minutes after the water stops boiling before using it. An exception to this temperature rule is the AeroPress. For reasons that I don't fully understand, this unique piece of equipment can make really delicious coffee within a range of water temperatures, even as low as 165ºF.

MEASURING

Accurately measuring coffee beans and water—by weight, instead of by volume—is incredibly crucial to making consistently tasty coffee. Unfortunately, this is where most home coffee-brewing failures begin.

I can't overstate the importance of purchasing a digital scale. It not only improves your ability to brew better coffee, but it makes measuring both beans and water much easier and more consistent. While it's certainly possible to measure both by volume, I personally feel like I'm blindfolded whenever I'm asked to make coffee without a scale. In addition to making it easier to recreate your desired cup of coffee every time, using a scale also ensures that you don't waste any beans. The size of whole coffee beans varies widely depending on variety and roast level, so a tablespoon of one style of bean yields a different amount of ground coffee than a tablespoon of another bean. On the other hand, 30 grams of any type of whole coffee bean will give you 30 grams of ground coffee every single time. Having accurate measurements also makes it easier to adjust a recipe's strength to suit your taste (see "Strength and Ratio," page 68).

Measuring water with a scale is also easy and far more accurate than measuring by volume. Burn this simple conversion into your memory: 1 milliliter of water conveniently weighs 1 gram. To make sure I consistently add the same amount of water to each brew, I place all of my equipment on the scale after weighing the beans, then I zero out (or "tare") the scale before adding the hot water.

STRENGTH AND RATIO

The strength of coffee (whether it tastes weak or strong) is often misunderstood as a characteristic of the coffee bean itself. However, strength has nothing to do with the type of bean used and everything to do with how much coffee is used. The ratio of bean to water you use when brewing ultimately determines the strength of the coffee. I recommend beginning with a 1:16 ratio, which is about 30 grams of coffee per 500 milliliters of water. Coffee strength is a personal preference, so you can alter this ratio depending on how strong you like your coffee—more ground coffee to water for a stronger brew, and less for something weaker.

In the previous section I discussed how difficult it is to accurately measure coffee without a scale. But many of you reading this book still won't immediately run out to buy one (you're forgiven). In the absence of a scale, using a tablespoon is the easiest way to estimate your coffee measurement. One level tablespoon of medium-ground coffee weighs about 5 grams. This isn't entirely accurate, and variances in grind size and roast level will affect the final outcome. (Also, because you need to grind coffee beans before measuring them with a tablespoon, this method will likely result in wasted beans.)

BREWING CONTROL

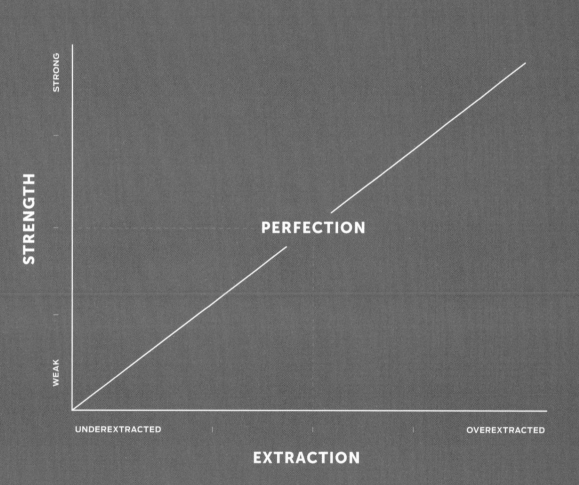

GRINDING

Once ground, the surface area of the coffee bean multiplies exponentially. While this helps water extract the coffee's flavors, it also makes the smaller particles far more sensitive to oxygen, which degrades all those wonderful aromatics and flavors. This is why it's important to begin with whole coffee beans instead of preground coffee. Grinding beans right before you brew them preserves their freshness and flavors.

The function of a coffee grinder is to break the beans down into the most uniformly sized particles as possible so water can extract the coffee's flavors evenly. Inconsistent grind size means that too much flavor will be extracted from smaller particles, leading to bitter coffee, while too little flavor will be extracted from larger particles, leading to sour coffee. It's difficult to clearly describe what grind size works best for a particular brewing method. The settings on every grinder are different, and it can be difficult to illustrate coffee grinds accurately. The important thing is to start in the ballpark using the grind chart on the opposite page and adjust according to your taste.

GRIND SIZE BY BREWING METHOD

COARSE

RAW SUGAR

French Press

Cold Brew

Chemex

Electric Drip

KOSHER SALT   MEDIUM

Pour Over

AeroPress

Moka Pot

GROUND CINNAMON

FINE

TASTING COFFEE

Coffee is the most complex beverage we drink. Really! It contains more aromatics than wine, and the number of aromas and flavors found in coffee ranges in the hundreds. A coffee's origin, the type of bean used, how the bean was processed and roasted, and even the brewing method determine the many different flavors you can experience in a cup of coffee. All of these variables can highlight different characteristics of a coffee, making each cup an opportunity to taste something new.

There are several ways that coffee professionals evaluate the quality and flavors in coffee, but the most common way is called "cupping." A cupping is a sensory exercise in which both the mouth and nose are used to compare different coffees. During a cupping, multiple styles of beans are brewed using the same set of variables, and then testers evaluate each one's characteristics, including fragrance, aroma, flavor, texture, acidity, and aftertaste. The primary taste sensations that a person can taste on his or her tongue are sweet, sour, bitter, salty, and savory (umami), but every person senses them at different degrees. The more experienced your palate becomes, the better you will be at identifying more specific and detailed traits of a coffee.

HOW TO SET UP A CUPPING

A cupping begins by measuring equal portions of different medium-coarse coffee grounds and placing them in a set of small identical bowls or wide-mouthed cups. The cups should be able to hold a volume between 7 and 9 ounces, and the amount of coffee used should be proportional to the amount of water that fits in each bowl (1:16 ratio). For example, a 7-ounce cup would need about 12 grams of ground coffee (roughly 2½ tablespoons). The important thing is to put the same amount of coffee and water in each cup.

Before adding water, first experience the fragrance of the unbrewed grounds. Pick up each cup, giving it a little shake, and place it under your nose. While breathing in the fragrance, focus on what you smell—flowers, fruit, chocolate, nuts, and so forth. If it helps, you can take notes to remember what was different about each coffee. Remember, a cupping is about exploring what you personally experience with each coffee, and everyone's sense of smell may pick up different aromas.

When you've finished evaluating the fragrance, set a timer for four minutes and pour hot water (200°F to 205°F) over the coffee grounds until each cup is filled almost to the brim. The coffee grounds will rise to the top and form a crust. During these four minutes, while the coffee is brewing, evaluate the aroma of the coffee by getting your nose as close to the crust as you can and inhaling. Note how the smell of the coffee has changed with the addition of water. You may find similarities to the unbrewed grounds, but you may also find something entirely new in the aroma.

Once the four minutes of brewing is complete, it's time to "break the crust." Use the back of a spoon to push through the coffee crust a few times and

gently mix the coffee into the water. If you place your nose close to the cup while breaking the crust, you'll experience a pleasant burst of aroma. Allow four to six more minutes to pass for the coffee to cool to a drinkable temperature. During this time you can use a spoon (or pair of spoons) to skim off any excess grounds that float on top of the coffee.

Finally, when the coffee has cooled, it's time to begin tasting. The ideal cupping spoon has a deep bowl, such as that of a soup spoon, so you can easily transport the coffee from the cup to your mouth. Dip your spoon into the first cup and bring the coffee to your lips. Slurp the coffee into your mouth, aerating it and covering your entire palate. Think about what you taste immediately, then during the middle and end of the slurp. Is the coffee sweet, fruity, citrusy, chocolaty, spicy, or smoky? What kind of body and texture do you experience, and how does the coffee feel in your mouth? Does it feel heavy or thin, clean, or tannic? At this point, you can spit the coffee into a cup or swallow it. Now consider what kind of aftertaste the coffee leaves in your mouth. Is it lingering or abrupt, juicy, or dry?

Repeat these steps with each cup of coffee while taking notes about how each tastes. (Rinse your spoon with hot water between each coffee, to avoid contamination and mixing the coffees.) Go back and try each coffee to see how the flavors evolve as the coffee continues to cool. You may find that some coffees taste better when they are cooler, while others change for the worse.

Cuppings are primarily reserved for professionals who work in the coffee industry, but it is becoming more common for local coffee roasters and cafés to offer public cuppings as a way for consumers to learn more about coffee. Hopefully this description leaves you feeling more comfortable with the process and will allow you to feel confident about participating in a cupping. However, comparing coffees doesn't require a cupping. You can just as easily brew multiple coffees with your method of choice and store them in several clean thermoses to keep them warm until you're ready to taste the coffees side-by-side. While this won't be as controlled as a cupping, it's an easy way to compare coffees. By tasting different coffees side-by-side, you can experience and evaluate their unique qualities while also training your palate to enjoy more of the subtleties in your daily cup.

MILK AND SUGAR

MILK

If you're one of the many people who prefers coffee with milk and sugar, rest assured that it's okay (I was once among you). As long as you still enjoy the way it tastes, you aren't ruining the coffee. However, many people drink their coffee this way out of sheer habit and haven't given high-quality black coffee a chance. If you recently switched from low-quality or dark-roasted coffee with lots of milk and/or sugar to a higher-quality brew, it might be worth giving black coffee another shot. Try tasting it before adding milk and sugar; you might be surprised at how naturally sweet and delicious a cup of properly brewed coffee tastes. The expectation of a smoky and bitter brew is based on most people's experience of drinking bad coffee. A well-roasted specialty coffee replaces the bitter characteristics of bad coffee with sweeter, more delicate flavors that don't require milk or sugar to be enjoyed. In fact, milk can actually mask the flavors for which you are paying extra money. All I ask is that you give it a try.

If you happen to be vegan or lactose intolerant but still want to add milk, there are several milk alternatives available that you may want to experiment with to create a creamy drink. Most people are aware of soy and almond milk, but you can also find milks made with rice, cashews, hemp, or oats, each of which adds different levels of creaminess to coffee as well as distinct flavors.

SUGAR

As with milk, I'm not going to judge you for using sugar. But, as with milk, I ask that you give high-quality coffee a taste before adding sweetener. Or consider experimenting with different kinds of sugar to add different levels and qualities of sweetness to your coffee. Personally I don't like sugar in my coffee because of how it affects the flavor, but for those who do, I've found that simple syrup made with raw sugar dissolves quickly and easily and adds subtle sweetness to both hot and cold coffee.

DRIP COFFEE

Drip coffee is a brewing method in which hot water is poured from above and gravity pulls the water through the coffee grounds and a filter into a vessel below. It creates a very balanced-tasting coffee that is both sweet and acidic, with a clean, smooth texture. This method includes everything from Mr. Coffee–style automatic machines to manual pour-over drippers. The filters used for drip coffee are usually made from paper, but there are also reusable options made from cloth and various metals.

POUR OVER

The pour-over method is a manual way of making drip coffee. By pouring the water over the grounds yourself (versus a machine doing it for you), you have better control of the water temperature and flow. This way you can be sure that all of the coffee grounds are properly saturated to better extract all of their flavors. This method also allows you to brew smaller amounts of coffee at a time, meaning that each cup is fresher and less coffee is wasted. There are many variations of pour-over drippers on the market, and although each one has its fans and critics, they all accomplish the same thing.

To begin, bring a kettle of water to a boil. While the water heats up, weigh out the proper amount of coffee beans and grind them on a medium setting (medium-coarse if you are using a Chemex). Place a filter into the pour-over dripper and rinse the filter with hot water. This reduces the paper taste the filter may add to your coffee, and it also preheats the brewing equipment. (Just be sure to empty the water before you brew.)

When you're ready to brew, place the pour-over dripper on top of a mug or carafe and set them both on top of your scale. (If you're using a Chemex, set it on the scale, too.) Pour the coffee grounds into the filter and lightly shake the dripper to level them. Zero (tare) the scale.

Start a timer and pour about 50 to 75 grams of water over the coffee grounds, or enough to make sure that all of the grounds are saturated. Allow the coffee to bubble up for about 30 seconds. This prewetting period is referred to as the "bloom," and it helps fresh coffee release carbon dioxide and preps the coffee grounds for better extraction.

After letting the grounds bloom for 30 seconds, continue pouring water over the coffee using a slow, steady stream. Begin in the center of the cone and slowly move the stream outward in a counterclockwise motion before circling back toward the center. Repeat this movement until you have added the proper amount of water. If the water level gets too high, take a break from pouring, but avoid leaving any coffee grounds sticking to the sides of the filter above the water line.

You should be done pouring water between the 2:00 and 2:30 minute marks on the timer. All of the water should finish passing through the dripper between the 3:00 and 3:30 minute marks. (If you are brewing a

batch larger than 500 milliliters, the water should take a bit longer to pass through the cone.) If the water takes too long to drip through, try using a coarser grind next time; if it drips through too quickly, try a finer grind (experiment until the coffee tastes the way you prefer). Pour into your cup and enjoy. (For a step-by-step pour-over coffee recipe, see page 98.)

ELECTRIC DRIP

To brew better coffee with an electric drip machine, all of the same principles from the pour-over method apply. Using freshly ground coffee, rinsing the filter, and weighing the coffee and water all make the coffee taste better.

To begin, weigh out the proper amount of coffee beans and grind them on a medium setting. Place a filter into the machine's filter holder and rinse it under hot tap water. This will reduce any papery taste that the filter may leave behind in your coffee. Pour the coffee grounds into the filter and place the filter holder back into the brewer.

Pour the proper amount of water into the machine's water reservoir. Be sure to use a clean vessel for the water so you don't contaminate the machine. When everything is in place, turn on the machine to begin the brew cycle. If the machine isn't getting all of the coffee grounds wet, use a spoon to stir the coffee and water together (this isn't possible with all styles of machines). Once the machine has finished the brew cycle, pour the coffee into your cup and enjoy. (For a step-by-step electric drip recipe, see page 102.)

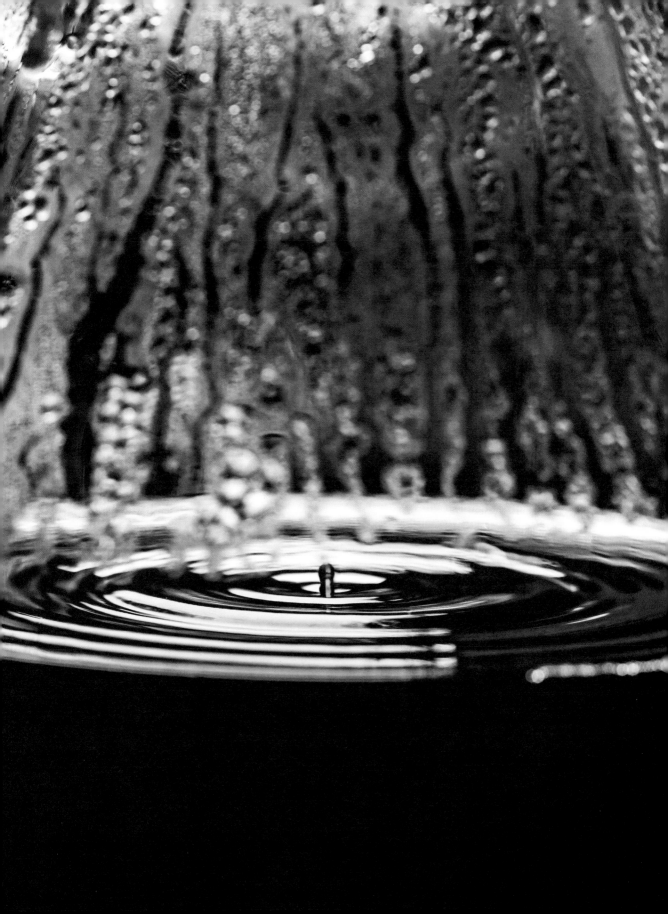

IMMERSION COFFEE

In the immersion brewing method, hot water and coffee grounds steep together for a set amount of time before the liquid is filtered and separated from the grounds. This method includes the French press, siphon (a complex beaker setup), cowboy coffee (the simplest and grittiest of brewing methods), percolators, and the AeroPress, which combines immersion and pressure. The metal filters commonly used for immersion brewing tend to yield coffee with a heavier texture, and methods like the French press and cowboy coffee usually leave some sediment in the brewing vessel and cup.

FRENCH PRESS

The French press is a relatively simple brewing method in which coffee grounds steep in hot water for a few minutes and then are separated from the brew using a plunger-style metal filter. The porous filter allows coffee oils and sediment to pass through into the brew, creating a full-bodied cup of coffee.

Before you start making coffee with a French press, you should preheat the press with hot water to ensure the water temperature remains stable and doesn't drastically change while you're brewing. While the pot is preheating, boil the water you will use for brewing. While the water heats up, weigh the proper amount of coffee beans for the amount of coffee you intend to brew and grind them on a medium-coarse setting. I suggest starting with a 1:14 (coffee to water) ratio and adjusting to your desired strength with future brews. Once the water has boiled, let it sit for about 2 minutes to drop down to the recommended temperature range of 200°F to 205°F.

Now that you're ready to begin brewing, empty the water used for preheating and pour the coffee grounds into the vessel. Set the French press on top of the scale and zero (tare) it before adding water. Start a timer for 4 minutes and begin pouring water over the coffee grounds, making sure they all get wet. Keep pouring until you have added the proper amount of water. (Remember that 1 milliliter of water = 1 gram, so 500 milliliters of water weighs 500 grams and 1000 milliliters weighs 1000 grams.) Set the lid on top of the French press (this will help keep the heat inside), but don't plunge it yet.

After 4 minutes have passed, remove the lid and use a spoon to break the crust of coffee grounds that formed on top of the water, but don't put the lid back on. Set the timer for 2 minutes and allow the coffee grounds to settle toward the bottom of the press. After 2 minutes, put the lid back on and slowly plunge the filter to the bottom of the pot. Pour the coffee right away or transfer it into another serving vessel to avoid overextraction and extra bitterness. Enjoy. (For a step-by-step French press coffee recipe, see page 105.)

PRESSURE COFFEE

In the pressure brewing method, high pressure forces hot water through coffee grounds and a filter. This method includes the moka pot, AeroPress, and espresso makers. Pressure-based methods are primarily used to speed up the extraction process, and the resulting coffee tends to be more concentrated with a heavier mouthfeel than drip coffee.

AEROPRESS

There are two primary ways to brew using the AeroPress: standard and inverted. I'll walk you through the inverted method because it's the method I prefer and it isn't explained in the AeroPress's instructions.

First, weigh out the proper amount of coffee beans and grind them on a medium-fine setting. I prefer a 1:12 (coffee to water) ratio with the AeroPress, but you can adjust according to your preferred strength. Next, connect the two long pieces of the AeroPress so the plunger rests about an inch inside the larger chamber. This allows you to stand the AeroPress upside down on its end. Rinse the AeroPress with a bit of hot water to preheat it; you can also put a filter in the filter cap and rinse it to prevent any paper residue from affecting the way your coffee tastes.

Now place the AeroPress onto the scale and pour the ground coffee into the top (the device comes with a funnel to help prevent spills). Zero out the scale, start a timer, and begin pouring water over the coffee grounds, making sure they all get wet, until you have poured in the proper amount of water.

After all the water has been added, give the coffee grounds a few quick stirs with a spoon, screw the filter cap securely into place (if you haven't done so already, be sure to put a filter in the cap), and let the coffee and water steep.

After 1 minute has passed, it's time to flip and press. Now comes the part that some might find tricky, and I recommend practicing a few times with an empty AeroPress so you get a feel for the technique. Place your cup or serving vessel upside down on top of the AeroPress with one hand while you hold the connecting joint of the AeroPress with your other. Now flip everything off the scale and onto the counter. Then slowly begin plunging the coffee into your cup; this should take about 30 seconds. Enjoy. (For a step-by-step AeroPress coffee recipe, see page 106.)

MOKA POT

When first brewing coffee with a moka pot, it's important to know that the size and design of each individual pot determines the amount of coffee and water you need to use. There isn't much room to experiment with the ratio with this method of brewing.

First, boil water in a separate kettle in order to prevent the moka pot from spending too much time on the stove and overheating. (Doing so also speeds up the brewing time and minimizes bitterness in the coffee.) While the water is coming to a boil, grind the coffee beans on a fine setting, but not quite as fine as that used for espresso. You need enough grounds to fill the filter basket to the brim. After pouring the coffee grounds into the filter basket, shake it slightly to level the coffee, but don't compact the grounds.

Pour the boiled water into the bottom chamber of the moka pot and fill it to just beneath the pressure-release valve, making sure not to cover the valve with water. Next, place the filter basket (filled with ground coffee) on top of the water chamber. Make sure the rubber gasket is in place on the top chamber, and screw the moka pot back together. Use a towel or hot pad when touching the bottom chamber because it is likely very hot from the water inside.

Place the moka pot over a medium-low heat source and wait for the steam to build up, which forces the water up through the coffee grounds. Be careful not to have the heat turned up too high. (I once had a moka pot explode and spray hot coffee all over my kitchen). After a few minutes, the steam pressure will start pushing brewed coffee up and out of the spout in the top chamber. If the coffee starts to spray, turn the heat down. If the coffee is struggling to drip out, turn the heat up a little bit.

Once you hear bubbling and hissing, the coffee is finished brewing. Remove the moka pot from the heat source and wrap a damp towel around the bottom chamber (or rinse it under cold water) to reduce the pressure and stop the brewing. Pour the coffee into your cup and enjoy. (For a step-by-step moka pot coffee recipe, see page 109.)

WHAT ABOUT ESPRESSO?

You've probably noticed that I'm not saying much about espresso in this book. There's a very good reason for that.

Espresso is the concentrated brew you get when hot water is forced through finely ground coffee at around 9 bars of atmospheric pressure. It was originally developed in Italy as a way to quickly brew an individual cup of coffee. For many people around the world, espresso and espresso-based drinks have come to symbolize the café experience, with smartly dressed baristas and high-end coffee machines. However, making good espresso at home is an expensive and complex endeavor that I recommend people avoid unless they are the most devoted of coffee aficionados. The amount of money, time, practice and effort needed to start pulling barista-quality shots of espresso is rarely worth the investment. After dropping a few thousand bucks (or more) on a good espresso machine and special espresso grinder, learning how to use both, letting the machine warm up every morning, and wasting a few shots to dial everything in, you might be able to make tasty espresso. And if you really want to dive into the process of making espresso at home, there are many great books dedicated to the topic (see "Resources," page 154).

I don't want to discourage you from pursuing your espresso-making dreams, but personally I'd rather focus on slow coffee at home, and when I want a shot of the potent stuff head down to my local café, where there's a trained barista and a $20,000 machine waiting.

COLD COFFEE

A hot cup of coffee is a wonderful part of most people's daily routine. But sometimes it's just too hot outside to drink hot coffee, or you always prefer cold beverages over warm ones. In recent years, cold coffee has enjoyed a surge in popularity, so much so that it's now a staple of most coffee shop menus, and bottled cold coffees can be found in most grocery stores. Before this cold-coffee boom, cafés commonly made iced coffee out of whatever hot-brewed coffee was left over at the end of the day. It was pretty vile stuff, but thankfully the options for cold coffee have progressed well beyond chilled day-old coffee. Almost all of the prepackaged, shelf-stable coffees are made using the cold-brew process; however, it's not the only way to make a cold-coffee beverage. In addition to chilling espresso drinks with ice and cold milk, there are two primary approaches to making cold-filter coffee: cold brew and flash chill. Each method has its fans and detractors, but there are distinct differences between each one that might help you decide which you prefer.

COLD BREW

Cold-brew coffee is made by either steeping coffee grounds and cold water together or slowly dripping cold water onto coffee grounds over a period of eight to twenty-four hours. The resulting coffee (from both methods) is smooth and has a much lower acidity than hot coffee and can be poured over ice, mixed with milk, or used to make various coffee drinks. One of the downsides of brewing with cold water is that some of the coffee's complex flavor compounds aren't fully extracted, resulting in a less-vibrant drink. However, for this same reason, cold-brew coffee is more shelf stable, allowing it to be made in large batches and stored for later use or bottled and sold for retail, making it a favorite among some coffee shops.

Steeped cold brew is easy to make, and you don't need any special equipment. You can use a French press, Mason jar, bucket—anything really—to mix coffee grounds with cold water. When the coffee has steeped long enough to extract the right amount of flavor, pour the mixture through a paper coffee filter to remove the grounds, and enjoy a smooth and clean coffee.

The cold-drip method requires a special pitcher, or tower, that slowly drips cold water over a column of coffee grounds at a rate of forty to sixty drops per minute. Seeing a cold-drip tower in action can be hypnotic, but it's not the most practical item for a home kitchen. Fans of the cold-drip method argue that it results in much smoother coffee, but I don't find the extra equipment worth the supposed benefits.

Cold brew is generally made as a strong concentrate that you dilute with water to achieve your desired strength. This approach allows you to make a lot more drinks with a much smaller pitcher, saving refrigerator space. The concentrate is incredibly potent and works well for making mixed coffee drinks (see "The Recipes," section, beginning on page 115). There are many companies that package and sell cold brew in both concentrate and ready-to-drink forms, but I've found that most of them use lower-quality beans and don't taste very good. You can easily achieve better results at home with your choice of high-quality beans.

FLASH CHILL

The flash-chill method involves brewing hot coffee and then rapidly cooling it to create a cold drink that better reflects the complexity and terroir of a specialty coffee. When you brew the coffee hot, you're able to extract the full range of flavors and aromatics, including the pleasant acidity that makes specialty coffee so delightful. By chilling the coffee quickly, you're also able to lock in the delicate flavors and prevent oxidation that can make the coffee taste rancid if it's cooled too slowly. There are several ways to approach this technique, but some of them require extra equipment, such as a heat exchanger, that most coffee brewers don't own. The easiest way to make flash-chilled coffee at home is with a method commonly referred to as "Japanese style."

Japanese-style cold coffee is achieved by brewing a concentrated hot coffee directly onto ice cubes, which simultaneously chill and dilute the coffee to the proper strength as they melt, resulting in a cold coffee that's ready to drink in just a few minutes. The key to this method is dividing the required amount of brew water for your desired recipe into proportional parts. Part of the water volume is heated and used to brew the concentrated coffee (as you normally would), while the remaining water volume is made up of ice. Simply fill the brewing vessel with the ice and let the hot coffee drip onto it while it is brewed. This technique works great with any pour-over dripper, an AeroPress, or even an electric drip machine.

When I make cold coffee, I prefer to use the flash-chilled/Japanese-style method because it provides coffee that (nearly) maintains the acidity and complexity of hot coffee. Brewing cold coffee this way is also faster because it doesn't require the advanced planning needed to make a batch of cold brew. The biggest downside to brewing cold coffee with the flash-chilled method is that it should be consumed the same day you make it. Many people enjoy the convenience that shelf-stable cold-brew coffee provides, but I would much rather drink something that is brewed fresh right before I drink it.

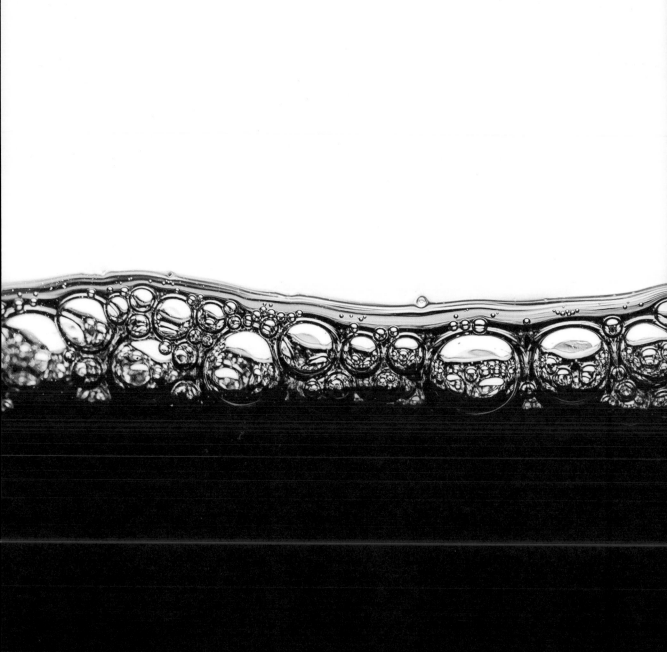

THE METHODS

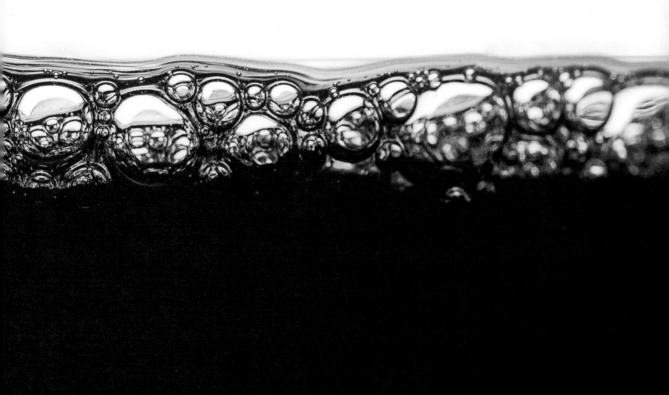

POUR OVER

The pour-over method is a manual way to make drip coffee. Pour-over coffee has become a ubiquitous brewing method at specialty coffee cafés, but long before the third wave and Mr. Coffee–era began, it was the original way to brew drip coffee at home. While making a pour over, you have better control of variables like water temperature, time, and coffee saturation. A pour over also allows you to brew anywhere from a single cup to several cups at the same time, ensuring you'll always have freshly brewed coffee.

WHAT YOU NEED

Fresh, whole coffee beans	Filter
Scale	Pour-over dripper
Grinder	Brewing vessel
Kettle	Timer
Water	Coffee cup(s)

RECOMMENDED COFFEE-TO-WATER RATIO (1:16)

For 1 to 2 cups: 20 g coffee beans (4 tablespoons ground) to 330 ml (11 ounces) water

For 2 to 3 cups: 30 g coffee beans (6 tablespoons ground) to 500 ml (16.5 ounces) water

For 3 to 4 cups: 45 g coffee beans (9 tablespoons ground) to 750 ml (25 ounces) water

Weigh the proper amount of coffee beans and grind them at a medium setting.

Heat a kettle of water to 200°F to 205°F (cool for about 2 minutes after boiling).

Place a filter into the dripper and rinse it with hot water. This will reduce any papery flavor the filter may add to the coffee and it also preheats the brewing vessel. Don't forget to empty the water from the brewing vessel.

Place the pour-over dripper on top of the brewing vessel and set them both on the scale. Zero (tare) the scale. Pour the coffee grounds into the filter and lightly shake the dripper to level them.

Zero the scale again. Start a timer and begin pouring about 50 to 75 grams of water over the coffee grounds, or enough to make sure all of the coffee is saturated. Allow the coffee to bloom for 30 seconds.

Pour water into the center of the coffee grounds, then slowly move the stream of water outward in a counterclockwise motion before circling back toward the center. Repeat this movement until you have added the proper amount of water. (Remember that 1 ml of water = 1 g, so 500 ml of water weighs 500 g.) If the water level gets too high, take a break from pouring. Try to avoid having coffee grounds stick to the filter above the water line.

Finish pouring water between the 2:00 and 2:30 minute mark on the timer. All of the water should finish passing through the coffee between the 3:00 and 3:30 mark. If the water is taking too long to pass through, try a coarser grind next time; if the water is passing through too quickly, try a finer grind. Experiment until the coffee tastes the way you prefer.

Pour into your favorite cup and enjoy.

CHEMEX

The Chemex is an hourglass-shaped carafe that holds the filter in place and doubles as the coffee brewer and vessel. People love the Chemex both for its design and the bright, clean coffee that pours through its thick paper filters, which retain more oil and sediment than other filters. The method for brewing with a Chemex is very similar to that of a pour-over dripper, though with an increased grind size and brewing time.

WHAT YOU NEED

Fresh, whole coffee beans
Scale
Grinder
Kettle
Water

Filter
Chemex
Timer
Coffee cup(s)

RECOMMENDED COFFEE-TO-WATER RATIO (1:16)

For 1 to 2 cups: 20 g coffee beans (4 tablespoons ground) to 330 ml (11 ounces) water

For 2 to 3 cups: 30 g coffee beans (6 tablespoons ground) to 500 ml (17 ounces) water

For 3 to 4 cups: 45 g coffee beans (9 tablespoons ground) to 750 ml (25 ounces) water

Weigh the proper amount of coffee beans and grind them at a medium-coarse setting.

Heat a kettle of water to 200°F to 205°F (cool for about 2 minutes after boiling).

Place a filter into the Chemex and rinse it with hot water. This will reduce any papery flavor the filter may add to the coffee and it also preheats the glass. Don't forget to empty the water from the Chemex.

Place the Chemex on the scale and zero (tare) the scale. Pour the coffee grounds into the filter and lightly shake the Chemex to level them.

Zero the scale again. Start a timer and begin pouring about 50 to 75 grams of water over the coffee grounds, or enough to make sure all of the coffee is saturated. Allow the coffee to bloom for 30 seconds.

Pour water into the center of the coffee grounds, then slowly move the stream of water outward in a counterclockwise motion before circling back toward the center. Repeat this movement until you have added the proper amount of water. (Remember that 1 ml of water = 1 g, so 500 ml of water weighs 500 g.) If the water level gets too high, take a break from pouring. Try to avoid having coffee grounds stick to the filter above the water line.

Finish pouring water between the 2:00 and 2:30 minute mark on the timer. All of the water should finish passing through the coffee between the 3:30 and 4:00 mark. If the water is taking too long to pass through, try a coarser grind next time; if the water is passing through too quickly, try a finer grind. Experiment until the coffee tastes the way you prefer.

Pour into your favorite cup and enjoy.

ELECTRIC DRIP

The electric drip machine is a very common way to make coffee in homes throughout the United States. These appliances brew drip coffee similar to a pour over, only they heat and dispense the water automatically over the coffee grounds. It's possible to brew great coffee with one of these machines as long as you are using one that has been certified by the Specialty Coffee Association (SCA).

WHAT YOU NEED

Fresh, whole coffee beans

Scale

Grinder

Filter

Water

Electric drip machine

Coffee cup(s)

RECOMMENDED COFFEE-TO-WATER RATIO (1:16)

For 1 to 2 cups: 20 g coffee beans (4 tablespoons ground) to 330 ml (11 ounces) water

For 2 to 3 cups: 30 g coffee beans (6 tablespoons ground) to 500 ml (16.5 ounces) water

For 3 to 4 cups: 45 g coffee beans (9 tablespoons ground) to 750 ml (25 ounces) water

Weigh the proper amount of coffee beans and grind them at a medium setting.

Place a filter into the filter basket and rinse it under hot tap water. This will reduce any papery flavor the filter may add to the coffee.

Pour the coffee grounds into the filter and place the filter basket in the machine.

Fill the machine with the proper amount of water.

Turn the machine on to begin the brew cycle. If the machine is not getting all of the coffee grounds wet, use a spoon to stir the coffee and water together (if your style of machine allows for this).

When the machine has finished the brew cycle, pour the coffee into your favorite cup and enjoy. (If the machine has a hot plate, avoid keeping the coffee on it for too long because the extended heat can cause bitterness and other unwanted flavors to develop.)

FRENCH PRESS

The French press is one of the easiest ways to make coffee at home and yields a full-bodied brew. After the water and coffee steep together for a period of time, a mesh filter is plunged through the coffee to separate the grounds before serving. The metal filter used by the French press allows coffee oils and sediment to pass through, which can enhance the flavor and add a rich body to the coffee.

WHAT YOU NEED

French press
Water
Fresh, whole coffee beans
Grinder
Kettle

Scale
Timer
Spoon
Coffee cup(s) or serving vessel

RECOMMENDED COFFEE-TO-WATER RATIO (1:14)

For 2 to 3 cups: 35 g coffee beans (7 tablespoons ground) to 500 ml (16.5 ounces) water

For 3 to 4 cups: 53 g coffee beans (10½ tablespoons ground) to 750 ml (25 ounces) water

For 4 to 5 cups: 70 g coffee beans (14 tablespoons ground) to 1 L (33 ounces) water

Fill the French press with hot water to preheat it. This will ensure that the water temperature doesn't drastically change while you're brewing.

Weigh the proper amount of coffee beans and grind them at a medium-coarse setting.

Heat a kettle of water to 200°F to 205°F (cool for about 2 minutes after boiling).

Empty the water used for preheating the French press and pour your coffee grounds into it.

Set the French press on top of your scale and zero (tare) it.

Set a timer for 4 minutes and begin pouring water over the coffee grounds, making sure they all get wet, until you have poured in the proper amount of water. Set the lid on top of the French press to keep the heat inside, but don't plunge the filter. (Remember that 1 ml of water = 1 g, so 500 ml of water weighs 500 g.)

After 4 minutes have passed, use the spoon to break the crust of coffee grounds that has formed at the top of the water, which will help the grounds sink into the coffee. Start a timer for 2 minutes.

After 2 minutes have passed, place the lid back onto the French press and slowly plunge the filter to the bottom of the pot.

Pour the coffee immediately into cups or transfer it to another serving vessel to avoid overextraction and extra bitterness. Enjoy.

AEROPRESS

The AeroPress is a unique brewing device that's great for making a single cup of coffee. It combines the simplicity of French press–style immersion brewing with the brightness and clean texture of drip coffee. Pressure is used to force the coffee through a filter, which helps reduce the brewing time, making it one of the fastest ways to brew a cup at home. This is my favorite method for using the AeroPress, but there are countless variations that can be found online.

WHAT YOU NEED

Fresh, whole coffee beans
Scale
Grinder
AeroPress
Kettle

Water
Paper AeroPress filter
Timer
Spoon or stir stick
Serving vessel (sturdy cup or another server)

RECOMMENDED COFFEE-TO-WATER RATIO (1:12)

For 1 cup: 18 g coffee beans (3.5 tablespoons ground) to 220 ml (7.5 ounces) water

Weigh the proper amount of coffee beans and grind them at a medium setting.

Connect the tube and plunger pieces of the AeroPress so the plunger rests about an inch inside the larger chamber. Stand the AeroPress upside down on its end.

Heat a kettle of water to 200°F to 205°F (cool for about 2 minutes after boiling).

Rinse the AeroPress with hot water to preheat it. Place a filter inside the filter cap and rinse it with water. This will reduce any papery flavor the filter may add to your coffee.

Set the AeroPress upside down onto the scale and pour the ground coffee into the top (the device comes with a funnel to help prevent spills). Zero (tare) the scale.

Start a timer and begin pouring water over the coffee grounds until you have added the proper amount of water. Make sure all of the coffee grounds get wet. (Remember that 1 ml of water = 1 g, so 500 ml of water weighs 500 g.) Give the coffee grounds a few quick stirs.

After 1 minute, hold the cup or serving vessel upside down on top of the AeroPress with one hand while holding the connecting joint of the AeroPress with your other. Now lift everything off the scale and flip it over onto the counter.

Slowly plunge all of the coffee into your cup or serving vessel. It should take about 30 seconds. Enjoy.

MOKA POT

The moka pot is an iconic Italian brewing device that, while not a true espresso maker, produces a strong and syrupy coffee that many espresso lovers enjoy. Although the moka pot is incredibly popular in Italy and many people around the world have one in their homes, it is a very finicky way to make coffee. It is difficult to control all of the brewing variables, and the results vary from one brew to the next.

WHAT YOU NEED

Kettle

Water

Moka pot

Fresh, whole coffee beans

Grinder

Coffee cup(s) or serving vessel

RECOMMENDED COFFEE-TO-WATER RATIO

The size and design of each individual moka pot determines the amount of coffee and water you use, so there isn't much room to experiment with this device.

Preboil water in a separate kettle. This will speed up the brewing time in the moka pot and prevent the coffee from overheating, which minimizes bitterness.

Fill the bottom chamber of the brewer with the preboiled water, up to, but not covering, the small pressure-release valve.

Grind the coffee beans at a fine setting (but not quite as fine as espresso). Fill up the metal filter basket with grounds, shaking it slightly to level the coffee. Do not tamp or compact the grounds.

Place the filter basket filled with coffee on top of the water chamber, making sure the rubber gasket is in place, and screw the moka pot back together. Use caution when touching the bottom chamber, as it will be very hot.

Place the moka pot over a medium-low heat source and wait for steam to build up and force water up through the coffee grounds. After a few minutes, the coffee should begin pouring out of the spout into the top chamber. If coffee is spraying out, lower the heat. If the coffee is barely dripping out, turn the heat up.

Once you begin to hear bubbling and hissing, the coffee is finished brewing. Remove the moka pot from the heat and wrap a damp towel around the bottom chamber or run it under cold water to reduce the pressure and stop the brewing.

Pour into your favorite cup and enjoy.

COLD-BREW CONCENTRATE

The cold-brew method makes a highly caffeinated drink that is less acidic than hot coffee but ultimately less complex in flavor. It can be diluted with water and poured over ice, combined with milk, or used to make various mixed coffee drinks. Cold brew concentrate can be made in large batches and refrigerated for up to a week. Many people enjoy the convenience of having a batch of cold brew available when the weather calls for something more refreshing than hot coffee.

WHAT YOU NEED

Fresh, whole coffee beans

Scale

Grinder

French press (or a large pitcher and fine-mesh sieve)

Water

Pour-over dripper

Filter

Serving vessel or storage container

RECOMMENDED COFFEE-TO-WATER RATIO (1:4)

For about 10 cups: 125 g coffee beans (1.5 cups ground) to 500 ml (16.5 ounces) water

For about 20 cups: 250 g coffee beans (3 cups ground) to 1 L (33 ounces) water

Weigh the proper amount of coffee beans and grind them at a medium-coarse setting.

Set the French press (or pitcher) on top of the scale and add the ground coffee. Zero (tare) the scale.

Fill the French press (or pitcher) with the proper amount of cold water. (Remember that 1 ml of water = 1 g, so 500 ml of water weighs 500 g.) Use a spoon to stir the coffee, making sure all of the grounds are wet.

Put the lid of the French press into place and press the filter down just enough to submerge the coffee below the water (or cover the pitcher). Let the coffee steep at room temperature for about 12 hours.

Slowly plunge the filter to the bottom of the French press. If you're using a pitcher, pour the coffee mixture through the fine-mesh sieve to remove the coffee grounds.

Place the pour-over dripper with a freshly rinsed filter over a serving vessel or storage container. Pour the cold-brew concentrate through the filter, letting the coffee drip through.

Before drinking, dilute the cold-brew concentrate with 1 part concentrate to 3 parts water (or to your preferred taste) and pour over ice. Both the diluted cold brew and undiluted concentrate can be used for several of the coffee drinks beginning on page 115. Cold-brew concentrate can be refrigerated for up to 1 week before it begins to degrade.

FLASH-CHILLED POUR OVER

The so-called Japanese style of making iced coffee, also known as flash chilling, yields a drink that better reflects the complexity of a freshly brewed cup of specialty coffee. When you brew the coffee hot and cool it rapidly, you're able to extract the full range of flavors and aromatics, including the good kinds of acidity that make specialty coffee so delightful. This style involves brewing concentrated hot coffee directly over a proportionate amount of ice, which melts and dilutes the final brew to the correct strength. You can also apply this technique to the AeroPress or any of the drip-style brewing methods to make a fresh and delicious batch of cold coffee.

WHAT YOU NEED

Fresh, whole coffee beans	Filter
Scale	Pour-over dripper
Grinder	Brewing vessel
Kettle	Timer
Water	Ice

RECOMMENDED COFFEE-TO-WATER AND ICE RATIO (1:16)

For 1 to 2 cups: 20 g coffee beans (4 tablespoons ground) to 220 ml (7.5 ounces) water and 110 g ice

For 2 to 3 cups: 30 g coffee beans (6 tablespoons ground) to 330 ml (11 ounces) water and 165 g ice

For 3 to 4 cups: 45 g coffee beans (9 tablespoons ground) to 500 ml (17 ounces) water and 250 g ice

Weigh the proper amount of coffee beans and grind them at a slightly finer than medium setting.

Heat a kettle of water to 200°F to 205°F (cool for about 2 minutes after boiling).

Place the dripper over a brewing vessel and place a filter inside the dripper. Rinse the filter with hot water. This will reduce any papery flavor the filter may add to the coffee and it also preheats the brewing vessel. Don't forget to empty the water from the brewing vessel.

Weigh out the proper amount of ice and place it in the brewing vessel.

Place the pour-over dripper on top of the brewing vessel and set them both on the scale. Zero (tare) the scale. Pour the coffee grounds into the filter and lightly shake the dripper to level them.

Zero (tare) the scale again. Start a timer and begin pouring about 50 to 75 grams of water over the coffee grounds, or enough to make sure all of the coffee is saturated. Allow the coffee to bloom for 30 seconds.

Pour water into the center of the coffee grounds, then slowly move the stream of water outward in a counterclockwise motion before circling back toward the center. Repeat this movement until you have added the proper amount of water. (Remember that 1 ml of water = 1 g, so 500 ml of water weighs 500 g.) If the water level gets too high, take a break from pouring. Try to avoid having coffee grounds stick to the filter above the water line.

Finish pouring water between the 2:00 and 2:30 minute mark on the timer. All of the water should finish passing through the coffee between the 3:00 and 3:30 mark. If the water is taking too long to pass through, try a coarser grind next time; if the water is passing through too quickly, try a finer grind. Experiment until the coffee tastes the way you prefer.

Pour into your favorite glass and enjoy. (Flash-chilled coffee is best consumed immediately.)

THE RECIPES

CAFÉ DE OLLA

As its Spanish name implies, "pot coffee" is a Mexican coffee drink traditionally prepared in earthenware pots (*ollas*), which are said to impart their own unique flavor, and sweetened with *piloncillo*, an unrefined brick of cane sugar with a strong molasses flavor. Here, I've tweaked the recipe for the American kitchen, though if you can find a clay *olla* or *piloncillo* at a Latin market, definitely use them.

TOOLS

Scale

Grinder

Saucepan

Whisk

French press or pour-over dripper and paper filter

Coffee cups

INGREDIENTS

30 g (⅓ cup) whole coffee beans

32 ounces (4 cups) water

½ cup (4 ounces) packed dark-brown sugar or piloncillo

1 cinnamon stick, plus more for garnish (optional)

Grind the coffee at a medium-coarse setting. In a small saucepan, bring the water, ground coffee, sugar, and cinnamon stick to a boil, whisking to dissolve the sugar. Remove from the heat and let steep, tasting frequently, for 5 to 10 minutes, or until brewed to your liking. Strain the coffee into cups through a pour-over dripper and paper filter (or use a French press), garnish with cinnamon sticks (if desired), and serve.

CAFÉ MOCHA

As with much of coffee history, the café mocha's origins are hard to definitively pin down. But we do know that the drink shares its name with both a Yemenite port and coffee variety found there that's said to have a distinctive chocolate flavor. As with any specialty coffee-based drink, this one is only going to taste as good as its ingredients, so don't hesitate to splurge on some fancy bean-to-bar chocolate.

TOOLS

Heatproof measuring cup

Mug

Spoon

INGREDIENTS

3 ounces (½ cup) bittersweet chocolate chips or pieces

2 ounces (¼ cup) boiling water

2 ounces (¼ cup) hot coffee

6 ounces (¾ cup) warm milk

Place the chocolate in a heatproof measuring cup and top with the boiling water. Stir until the chocolate has melted. Pour 3 tablespoons of the chocolate ganache into a mug and add the coffee. Top with the warm milk, stir, and serve.

IRISH COFFEE

This boozy winter drink is said to have been invented in an Irish airport in the early 1940s after a New York–bound flight returned to the gate due to stormy weather. To warm the cold and haggard passengers after their aborted trip, Joe Sheridan, a chef at the airport's restaurant, mixed strong coffee with Irish whiskey and brown sugar, then topped the drink with a layer of heavy cream. Traditional recipes don't call for whipping the cream first, but I find that lightly whipped cream makes for a thick, creamy cap that will stay in place atop the drink as you sip. I've also had lots of success making un-Irish versions of this drink with other styles of whiskey and even aged rum.

TOOLS

Mixing bowl

Whisk

Glass mug

INGREDIENTS

2 ounces (¼ cup) heavy cream

2 ounces (¼ cup) Irish whiskey

6 ounces (¾ cup) hot coffee

2 teaspoons (8 g) brown sugar

Freshly grated cinnamon, for garnish (optional)

In a mixing bowl, whisk the cream until thickened slightly (stop before you hit soft peaks; the cream should still be loose and runny) and refrigerate until ready to use.

Pour the whiskey, coffee, and sugar into a heated glass mug and stir to dissolve the sugar. Top with a layer of the whipped cream, grate some cinnamon over the top (if desired), and serve.

VIETNAMESE ICED COFFEE

The Vietnamese *ca phe sua da* means "coffee, milk, ice" and dates back to the nineteenth century, when French Catholic priests introduced coffee to Vietnam. This is one coffee drink that benefits from a darker roast, which can stand up to the intense sweetness of the condensed milk. Many make theirs with a blend of coffee and chicory, but I like the robust flavors of medium-dark roast beans (try a specialty espresso blend). If you don't have a Vietnamese drip filter (they're easy to find online and in Asian groceries) or don't want to buy one, you can brew a strong pot of coffee and combine it with the milk over ice in the glass.

TOOLS

Tall glass

Vietnamese drip filter

Scale

Grinder

Water kettle

INGREDIENTS

1 ounce (2 tablespoons) sweetened condensed milk, well stirred

25 g (about ¼ cup) whole medium-dark roast coffee beans

8 ounces (1 cup) water

Ice cubes

Pour the condensed milk into a glass. Place a Vietnamese drip filter on top of the glass and remove the lid and upper screen. Grind the beans at a medium-fine setting and add to the filter, tapping the container so the grounds settle evenly. Fix the upper screen over the coffee (don't pack the grounds). Depending on the style of the filter, you may need to screw on the screen.

Heat a kettle of water to 200°F to 205°F (cool for about 2 minutes after boiling). Pour a small amount of water over the grounds to let them bloom. Wait about 30 seconds, then add enough water to reach the top of the filter. Cover the filter and let the coffee drip through (it should take about 4 minutes).

Remove the filter and set it aside. Add ice to the glass, stir to combine the coffee and milk, and serve.

NEW ORLEANS COLD BREW

MAKES 2 CUPS OF CONCENTRATE (ENOUGH FOR 6 DRINKS)

Throughout history, chicory has been used in times of coffee bean shortages or economic hardship to stretch out precious coffee beans. The practice of adding chicory to coffee originated in France during a Napoleon-era blockade and was popularized stateside by French settlers in New Orleans when the city's ports were cut off during the Civil War. The dried and ground root of the blue-flowered chicory plant exhibits some flavors similar to coffee beans, as well as a distinctive roasted nuttiness that works in both hot- and cold-brewed coffees. You can find ground chicory root at many spice shops or specialty markets.

TOOLS

Scale

Grinder

French press or pitcher
Spoon

Fine-mesh sieve

Pour-over dripper and paper filter

Serving vessel or storage container

INGREDIENTS

125 g (about 1½ cups) whole coffee beans

12 g (1½ tablespoons) dried chicory root

16 ounces (2 cups) water

Ice cubes

Milk (optional)

Simple syrup or maple syrup (optional; see Note)

Grind the beans at a medium-coarse setting and add the grounds to the French press (or pitcher) along with the chicory. Add the water and use a spoon to lightly stir the mixture, making sure all of the grounds are wet. Put the lid of the French press into place and press the filter down just enough to submerge the coffee below the water (or cover the pitcher). Let the coffee steep at room temperature for about 12 hours.

Slowly plunge the filter to the bottom of the French press. If you're using a pitcher, pour the coffee mixture through a fine-mesh sieve to remove the coffee grounds. Place the pour-over dripper with a freshly rinsed filter over a serving vessel or storage container. Pour the cold-brew concentrate through the filter, letting the coffee drip through. Before drinking, dilute the cold-brew concentrate using 1 part concentrate to 3 parts water and/or milk (or to your preferred taste) and serve over ice, sweetened with simple syrup or maple syrup if desired. The concentrate can be refrigerated for up to 1 week before it begins to degrade.

Note: To make simple syrup, dissolve 1 part granulated sugar in 1 part simmering water and let cool.

COLD-BREW SHAKERATO

The café shakerato is a magic trick. Despite the absense of milk or cream, when shaken with ice, coffee and simple syrup form a cold drink with a creamy layer on top. The shakerato has been trendy in Italy for some time and is catching on in America and elsewhere; my version substitutes the usual espresso for cold coffee, resulting in a refreshing drink that's easy to make at home.

TOOLS

Cocktail shaker

Strainer

Short glass

INGREDIENTS

Ice cubes

6 ounces (¾ cup) cold coffee (flash-chilled pour over or diluted cold-brew concentrate, page 110)

½ ounce (1 tablespoon) simple syrup (see Note)

Fill a cocktail shaker with ice. Add the coffee and simple syrup and shake vigorously until the sides of the shaker are very cold, about 15 seconds. Strain into a short glass and serve.

Note: To make simple syrup, dissolve 1 part granulated sugar in 1 part simmering water and let cool.

COLD BREW & BITTERS

This is a nonalcoholic (unless you count the bitters) version of the old fashioned. It's perfect for those times when you want to look and feel like you're enjoying a cocktail but would rather get picked up with caffeine rather than laid out by whiskey.

TOOLS

Rocks glass

Spoon

INGREDIENTS

1 large ice cube

3 ounces (⅜ cup) cold coffee (flash-chilled pour over or diluted cold-brew concentrate, page 110)

3 dashes Angostura bitters

½ ounce (1 tablespoon) demerara syrup (see Note)

Orange twist, for garnish

Place a large ice cube in a rocks glass and add the coffee, bitters, and syrup. Stir briefly, garnish with the orange twist, and serve.

Note: To make demerara syrup, dissolve 1 part demerara sugar in 1 part simmering water and let cool.

JUMPING JULEP

MAKES 1 DRINK

This is about as fancy as cold brew gets: dressed up for the races with mint-infused simple syrup and a silver tin. It's just the thing to drink after a bourbon-based julep or two, or you can even swap bourbon for about half of the coffee in this recipe.

TOOLS

Saucepan

Fine-mesh sieve

Mixing spoon

Julep tin

INGREDIENTS

½ cup (120 g) sugar

4 ounces (½ cup) water

¾ cup packed mint leaves

Crushed ice

4 ounces (½ cup) cold-brew concentrate (page 110)

Mint bouquet, for garnish

First, make the mint syrup. In a small saucepan, bring the sugar, water, and mint to a boil, stirring until the sugar is dissolved. Simmer the syrup for 2 minutes, then strain through a fine-mesh sieve, pressing on the solids with a spoon. Let cool, then refrigerate until ready to use.

Fill a julep tin with crushed ice. Add 1 teaspoon mint syrup and the cold-brew concentrate and stir until the side of the tin turns frosty. Mound more crushed ice on top of the drink, garnish with the mint, and serve.

COFFEE & COLA

In the mid 2000s, Coca-Cola released a coffee-flavored soda called Coca-Cola Blāk. The product never caught on and was only in circulation for a couple of years, but the idea lives on in this sophisticated soda. Use whatever brand of cola you prefer, but my best results have been with more complex artisanal sodas.

TOOLS

Tall glass

Mixing spoon

INGREDIENTS

Ice cubes

1½ ounces (3 tablespoons) cold-brew concentrate (page 110)

½ ounce (1 tablespoon) simple syrup (see Note)

3 ounces (¾ cup) cola

3 ounces (¾ cup) club soda

Lime wheel, for garnish

Fill a tall glass with ice cubes. Add the cold-brew concentrate and simple syrup and stir briefly. Top with the cola and club soda, garnish with the lime wheel, and serve.

Note: To make simple syrup, dissolve 1 part granulated sugar in 1 part simmering water and let cool.

KAFFELEMONAD

Coffee lemonade—coffee's answer to the Arnold Palmer—has its roots in Sweden, and is now popping up in specialty coffee bars across America. Nothing is better on a hot summer afternoon when you want a refreshing pick-me-up with less caffeine. You can also make a large batch by swapping ounces for cups in the recipe.

TOOLS

Tall glass

Spoon

INGREDIENTS

Ice cubes

3 ounces (¾ cup) cold coffee (flash-chilled pour over, diluted cold-brew concentrate, page 110)

2 ounces (¼ cup) fresh lemon juice

1 ounce (2 tablespoons) simple syrup (see Note)

2 ounces (¼ cup) club soda

Lemon wedge, for garnish

Fill a tall glass with ice cubes. Add the coffee, lemon juice, and simple syrup and stir well. Top with club soda, garnish with the lemon wedge, and serve.

Note: To make simple syrup, dissolve 1 part granulated sugar in 1 part simmering water and let cool.

COLD-BREW G&T

The coffee and tonic—a bracing blend of cold-brew coffee (or espresso) and tonic water—has been appearing on trendy café menus over the past couple of years. It's a fine drink on its own, though many baristas enhance the formula with fruit syrups, citrus, herbs and other add-ins. My favorite riff on this trendy drink is a boozy one that, not surprisingly, takes its inspiration from the most famous tonic-based cocktail: the gin and tonic.

TOOLS

Tall glass

Mixing spoon

INGREDIENTS

Ice cubes

1½ ounces (3 tablespoons) gin

1½ ounces (3 tablespoons) cold-brew concentrate (page 110)

4 ounces (½ cup) tonic water

Lemon wedge, for garnish

Fill a tall glass with ice cubes. Add the gin and cold-brew concentrate and stir briefly. Top with the tonic water, garnish with the lemon wedge, and serve.

AMERICANO-AMERICANO

This invigorating concoction combines two of my favorite drinks: iced coffee and the Americano, a classic Italian cocktail made with Campari and sweet vermouth (so named because it was a hit with American expats during Prohibition). I've enjoyed this hybrid drink as a pick-me-up during brunch, as a low-alcohol refresher on summer afternoons, and on either end of a big meal. If you don't have any cold-brew coffee on hand, you can make this drink with an iced Americano (espresso and water).

TOOLS

Mixing glass

Mixing spoon

Cocktail strainer

Highball glass

INGREDIENTS

1 ounce (2 tablespoons) Campari

1 ounce (2 tablespoons) sweet vermouth

1 ounce (2 tablespoons) cold-brew concentrate (page 110)

Ice cubes

Club soda

Orange wheel, for garnish

In a mixing glass, combine the Campari, vermouth, and coffee. Fill the mixing glass with ice and stir the drink until cold, about 20 seconds. Strain into an ice-filled highball glass and top with club soda. Stir once or twice, garnish with the orange wheel, and serve.

CASCARA SPRITZER

MAKES 1 DRINK

Cascara is a tealike drink made from the dried skins (or husks) of the coffee cherry left behind after processing. When brewed, this by-product makes a floral, fruity (and caffeinated) drink that's delicious on its own. Here, we make a concentrated syrup from the cascara that forms the basis of a bright, refreshing spritzer. While cascara can be hard to come by in stores, some roasters—including Slingshot Coffee, 44 North, and 49th Parallel—sell cascara online.

TOOLS

Kettle

Fine-mesh sieve

Tall glass

INGREDIENTS

10 ounces (1¼ cups) water

½ cup (about 40 g) cascara

3 tablespoons (about 36 g) sugar (preferably demerara)

Ice cubes

8 ounces (1 cup) club soda

First, make the cascara syrup. Heat a kettle of water to 200ºF to 205ºF (cool for about 2 minutes after boiling). Place the cascara and sugar in a heatproof container and add the water. Stir until the sugar has dissolved and let steep for 5 minutes. Strain the mixture into another container, cover, and refrigerate until ready to use.

To make the cascara spritzer, fill a tall glass with ice cubes and add 1 ounce of syrup. Top with the club soda and serve.

COFFEE LIQUEUR

There are plenty of coffee liqueurs to be found on liquor store shelves, but I've found the coffee flavor in most of them uninteresting at best. It's much easier (and cheaper!) to make your own. You can also substitute aged rum or bourbon for the vodka.

TOOLS

Saucepan

Whisk

Bottles or Mason jars

Pour-over dripper and paper filter

Fine-mesh sieve

INGREDIENTS

4 ounces (½ cup) water

½ cup (96 g) turbinado sugar

8 ounces (1 cup) vodka

½ cup (40 g) coarsely ground coffee beans

½ vanilla bean, split and seeds scraped

In a small saucepan, bring the water to a simmer and add the sugar. Turn off the heat and whisk until the sugar has dissolved. Let cool before using.

In a bottle or Mason jar, combine 4 ounces of the turbinado syrup with the vodka, coffee grounds, vanilla seeds and bean. Cover and infuse at room temperature for 24 hours. Line a pour-over dripper with a paper coffee filter and wet the filter. Place a small fine-mesh sieve over the dripper and strain the coffee liqueur through the sieve and paper filter into a clean bottle or jar.

COFFEE OLD FASHIONED

If you've gone through all the trouble of making coffee liqueur, you deserve a drink to put it to good use. Here, the intensely flavored spirit shares the glass with bourbon and bitters (two of the three ingredients in a classic old fashioned), while the sweetness of the liqueur eliminates the need for any additional sugar.

TOOLS

Mixing glass

Mixing spoon

Cocktail strainer

Rocks glass

INGREDIENTS

Ice cubes, plus 1 large ice cube

1½ ounces (3 tablespoons) bourbon

1 ounce (2 tablespoons) Coffee Liqueur (page 143)

2 dashes Angostura bitters

Orange twist, for garnish

Fill a mixing glass with ice and add the bourbon, coffee liqueur, and bitters. Stir until very cold, then strain into a rocks glass over 1 large ice cube. Garnish with the orange twist and serve.

RED-EYE MANHATTAN

Is it ever appropriate to drink a Manhattan at brunch? When the drink contains a dose of cold brew coffee, why not? As evidenced by the Irish Coffee (page 120) and the Jumping Julep (page 131), coffee and whiskey are fabulous bedfellows. In addition to midday drinking, this complex cocktail is also a great postprandial beverage for those who want a hit of caffeine after a meal.

TOOLS

Mixing glass

Mixing spoon

Cocktail strainer

Coupe

INGREDIENTS

Ice cubes

2 ounces (¼ cup) rye

1 ounce (2 tablespoons) cold-brew concentrate (page 110)

1 ounce (2 tablespoons) sweet vermouth

2 dashes Angostura bitters

Fill a mixing glass with ice. Add the rye, cold-brew concentrate, vermouth, and bitters. Stir until very cold, then strain into a coupe and serve.

GUINNESS AFFOGATO FLOAT

A scoop of vanilla gelato doused with a shot of hot espresso is my favorite two-ingredient dessert. Several scoops of gelato drowning in high-quality coffee and malty, chocolatly Guinness stout? Even better.

TOOLS

Ice cream scoop

Tall glass

Spoon and straw

INGREDIENTS

4 scoops (about 1½ cups) vanilla gelato (or vanilla ice cream)

2 ounces (¼ cup) hot strong-brewed coffee

4 ounces (½ cup) Guinness stout

Fill a tall glass with the gelato. Add the coffee and top with the Guinness. Serve with a spoon and straw.

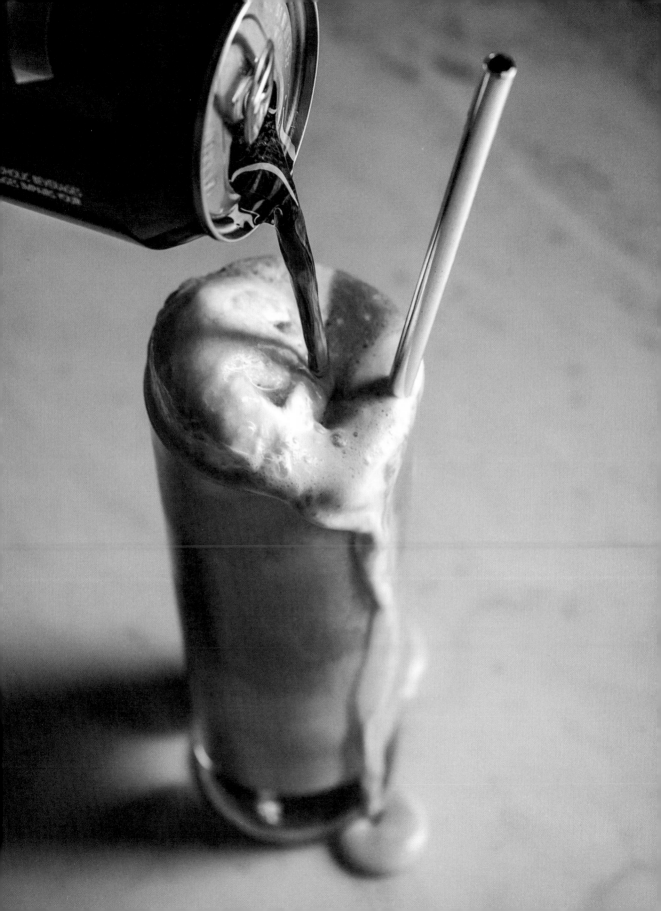

COFFEE MILKSHAKE

MAKES 1 DRINK

Making a coffee milkshake is as easy as blending coffee ice cream with milk, but most coffee ice cream isn't made with great beans. To improve the coffee flavor, I like to instead combine homemade cold-brew concentrate with high-quality vanilla ice cream. For an extra hit of flavor, finely grate a coffee bean over the finished drink.

TOOLS

Blender

Ice cream scoop

Tall glass

Grater

INGREDIENTS

4 ounces (½ cup) whole milk

2 ounces (¼ cup) cold-brew concentrate (page 110), or more to taste

4 scoops (about 1½ cups) vanilla ice cream

Freshly grated coffee bean, for garnish (optional)

Pour the milk and cold-brew concentrate into a blender. Add the ice cream and blend until smooth, adding more cold-brew concentrate for a stronger coffee flavor. Top the drink with a freshly grated coffee bean, if desired, and serve.

GLOSSARY

Acidity – Chemical compounds in coffee that are responsible for most of the desired fruit-like flavors.

AeroPress – A syringe-like device that makes a single cup of coffee using properties of both immersion and pressure brewing.

Arabica – The most common species of commercially grown coffee bean; it is considered higher in quality than robusta, and is the primary species used in specialty coffee.

Blend – A mixture of coffee beans with more than one origin.

Bloom – Prewetting the coffee grounds to release excess gas and to aid the brewing process.

Body – The texture and viscosity (perceived thickness) of a coffee experienced on your palate. Also known as "mouthfeel."

Brew ratio – The relational measurement of coffee grounds to water that determines the strength of brewed coffee.

Brew time – The amount of time that water is in contact with the coffee grounds while brewing.

Burr grinder – A machine that uses two metal discs or nested cones to crush coffee beans into uniform particles.

Chaff – The dry papery remains of the coffee bean's silver skin that comes off during roasting.

Commodity coffee – Coffee that is sold on the global market with no regard for its quality or traceability.

Crack (first) – A critical point in the roasting process when coffee beans expand to release gases trapped inside; an audible cracking sound occurs when the beans' temperature reaches around 380ºF.

Crack (second) – A point in the roasting process when coffee beans are roasted very dark and expand a second time, producing another cracking sound around 435ºF.

Cupping – A method of brewing, smelling, and tasting several different coffees side-by-side for comparison and evaluation.

Degas – A process that occurs for a few days after roasting in which coffee beans expel a lot of gases, such as carbon dioxide, which can affect their flavors.

Direct trade – An unregulated term implying that coffee roasters buy coffee through direct relationships with coffee farmers.

Drip coffee – A method of coffee brewing in which water passes through coffee grounds and a filter with the aid of gravity.

Extraction – The amount of flavor removed from coffee grounds during the brewing process.

Fair trade – A certification provided by several nonprofit organizations to guarantee better pricing for coffee farmers who meet certain criteria regarding safety, sustainability, and community investments.

French press – A device used for steeping coffee grounds and water together before a metal filter is plunged down to separate them. French press coffee is an example of immersion brewing.

Green coffee – The name for coffee beans in their processed but unroasted form.

Grind size – The size of ground coffee particles adjusted for proper extraction during brewing.

Honey process (semiwashed or pulped natural) – A method of processing coffee that involves allowing the mucilage to dry on the seed before the beans are milled.

Immersion brewing – A category of brewing methods that involve steeping coffee grounds in water for a set amount of time.

Lot – A selection of coffee that has been sorted and separated into a specific grouping.

Moka pot – An Italian device that uses steam pressure to brew a thicker style of coffee similar to espresso.

Mucilage – A sticky, honey-like gel that is left on the bean after the fruit is removed.

Mouthfeel – See "body."

Natural process (dry or sun-dried) – A method of processing coffee that involves allowing the whole coffee cherries to dry before the beans are separated from the fruit.

Overextracted – When too much flavor has been removed from the coffee grounds, including the undesirable ones, resulting in a bitter and unpleasant-tasting coffee.

Parchment – A thin, papery shell that encases the coffee beans and is removed at a mill before the beans are exported to coffee roasters.

Peaberry – A rare genetic mutation that occurs in some coffee cherries, in which only one bean develops instead of two. These beans are sometimes sorted and sold as a special offering.

Pour over – A manual method of making drip coffee using a cone-shaped dripper, a filter, and a kettle to pour water over the coffee grounds.

Pressure brewing – A category of brewing methods that use pressure to force water through the coffee grounds to extract flavor.

Pulp – The discarded portion of a coffee cherry that includes the skin and most of the fruit.

Roasting – The process of heating green coffee beans to induce various chemical reactions that develop the flavors that are extracted during brewing.

Roast profile – A set of data created by a roaster to develop a specific coffee bean to his or her desired roast level.

Robusta – A cheaper, lower-quality species of coffee that grows better at lower altitudes and is more resistant to disease than arabica coffee.

Single origin – Coffee beans from a distinct location, which can be as specific as the country, region, mill, farm, or lot.

Specialty coffee – Coffee that meets a certain industry standard, is free of defects, and is produced with quality and flavor in mind to display the characteristics of a specific origin.

Strength – How intense or weak a coffee tastes depending on the brew ratio used.

Terroir – The specific environmental and geographic characteristics of a place—including the soil composition, weather, and elevation—that influence the flavor of coffee beans grown there.

Underextracted – When too little desirable flavor has been removed from the coffee grounds, resulting in a sour and weak-tasting coffee.

Variety – The numerous subspecies within the coffee family that have unique characteristics that impact how they are grown and how they taste.

Washed process (wet) – A method of processing coffee that involves squeezing the beans from the cherries before soaking them in water (to remove the sticky mucilage), and then drying the beans.

RESOURCES

RECOMMENDED READING

Ellis, Markman. *The Coffee House: A Cultural History.* Orion Publishing, 2004.

Freeman, James. *The Blue Bottle Craft of Coffee: Growing, Roasting, and Drinking, with Recipes.* Ten Speed Press, 2012.

Hoffmann, James. *The World Atlas of Coffee.* Firefly Books, 2014.

Kingston, Lani. *How to Make Coffee: The Science Behind the Bean.* Abrams, 2015.

Pendergrast, Mark. *Uncommon Grounds: The History of Coffee & How It Transformed Our World.* Basic Books, 2010.

Rao, Scott. *Espresso Extraction: Measurement & Mastery.* Scott Rao Coffee Books, 2013.

Ukers, William Harrison. *All About Coffee.* The Tea and Coffee Trade Journal, 1922.

Weissman, Michaele. *God in a Cup: The Obsessive Quest for the Perfect Coffee.* Houghton Mifflin Harcourt, 2008.

Wendelboe, Tim. *Coffee with Tim Wendelboe.* Everyone, 2014.

BLOGS AND ONLINE RESOURCES

Dear Coffee, I Love You. (dearcoffeeiloveyou.com)

Barista Hustle (baristahustle.com)

Jim Seven (jimseven.com)

Specialty Coffee Association (sca.coffee)

Sprudge (sprudge.com)

ONLINE SOURCES FOR TOOLS AND BEANS

Brian's curated Amazon store (shop.dearcoffeeiloveyou.com)

Clive Coffee (clivecoffee.com)

Prima Coffee (prima-coffee.com)

MistoBox – customizable coffee subscription (mistobox.com)

BRIAN'S FAVORITE COFFEE ROASTERS

AKA Coffee – Oakland, CA (aka.coffee)

Counter Culture Coffee – Durham, NC (counterculturecoffee.com)

George Howell Coffee – Acton, MA (georgehowellcoffee.com)

Heart Coffee – Portland, OR (heartroasters.com)

Intelligentsia Coffee – Chicago, IL (intelligentsiacoffee.com)

Madcap Coffee – Grand Rapids, MI (madcapcoffee.com)

Onyx Coffee Lab – Springdale, AR (onyxcoffeelab.com)

Parlor Coffee – Brooklyn, NY (parlorcoffee.com)

Ritual Coffee – San Francisco, CA (ritualroasters.com)

Ruby Colorful Coffees – Nelsonville, WI (rubycoffeeroasters.com)

Spyhouse Coffee – Minneapolis, MN (spyhousecoffee.com)

Slate Coffee – Seattle, WA (slatecoffee.com)

Supercrown Coffee – Brooklyn, NY (supercrown.coffee)

Tandem Coffee – Portland, ME (tandemcoffee.com)

Variety Coffee – Brooklyn, NY (varietycoffeeroasters.com)

Verve Coffee – Santa Cruz, CA (vervecoffee.com)

INDEX

ACKNOWLEDGMENTS

Everything that led up to the creation of this book has been made possible by the inspiration, knowledge, and friendship of the many fantastic coffee professionals I have met over the years.

Thank you to everyone I have had the opportunity to learn from along the way. I've had memorable conversations, arguments, and discussions with you all at some point that influenced my thoughts and perspective on coffee. Further, you continue to inspire me with your own work:

The Coffee Common team—Stephen Morrissey, Peter Giuliano, Kyle Glanville, Tim Williams, Brent Fortune, Sean Bonner, and all of the baristas who took part. Anne Lunnel, Charles Nystrand, James Hoffmann, Tim Wendelboe, Klaus Thomsen, Ben Kaminsky, Aleco Chigounis, Matt Perger, Charles Babinski, Tim Varney, Colin Harmon, Gwilym Davies, Geoff Watts, Oliver Strand, Michael Phillips, Nicolas Clerc, Joanna Alm, Patrik Rolf Karlsson, Kris Schackman, Elin Conradsson, Stephen Leighton, Jesse Kahn, Katie Carguilo, Erin Meister, Nick Cho, Tony Kenecny, Jay Lijewski, Kim Staalman, Seth Mills, Sam Meis, and Kalle Freese.

Thanks for the support of my business partners, John Laird and Björg Brend Laird.

Thanks to Penny for her endless patience.

And a thank you to the team who helped make this book awesome: Dovetail Press, Lizzie Munro for her fantastic photography, both Nick Fauchald and James Lainsbury for their editing prowess, Supercrown Coffee for sharing their lovely facilities, and Baratza for taking care of our grinder needs.

ABOUT THE AUTHOR

Since 2000, Brian W. Jones's experience with coffee has involved working as a barista, being a home-coffee enthusiast, serving coffee at TED conferences and the Sundance Film Festival, competing in and organizing coffee competitions, and cofounding a coffee-roasting company in Oakland, California. Brian has written about coffee and its intersection with culture and design since 2009 on his website Dear Coffee, I Love You, and he has given talks about coffee around the world—from Seattle to Stockholm to Shanghai. As a designer and writer, Brian uses both mediums to help others better appreciate and enjoy their daily coffee.

Published by Dovetail Press in Brooklyn, New York, a division of Assembly Brands LLC.

For details or ordering information, contact the publisher at the address below or email **info@dovetail.press.**

Dovetail Press
42 West Street #403
Brooklyn, NY 11222
www.dovetail.press

Library of Congress Cataloging-in-Publication data is on file with the publisher.

ISBN: 978-0-9898882-2-6

First Edition

Printed in China

10 9 8 7 6 5 4 3

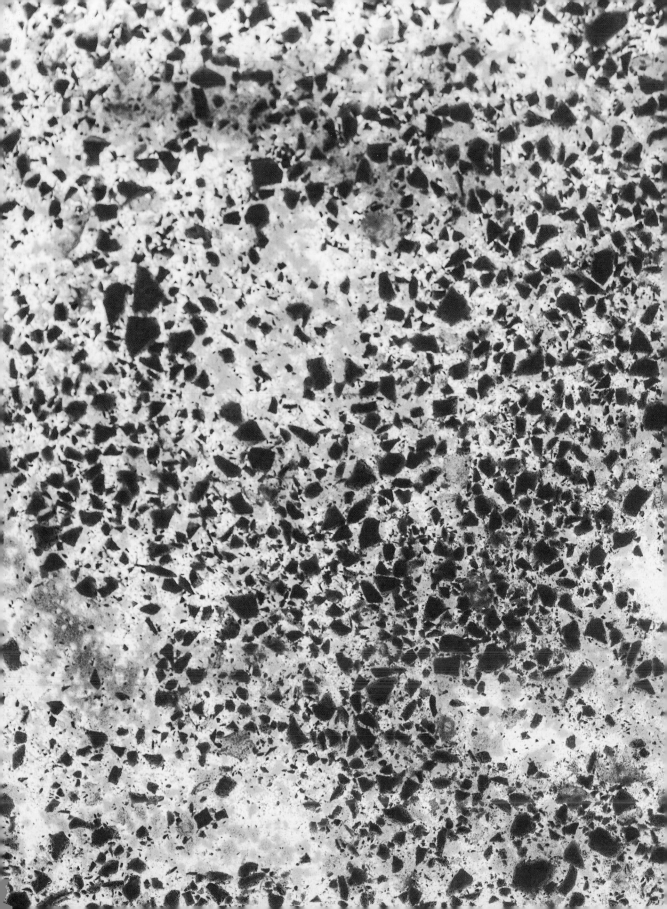